MODERN
SEA POWER

An Introduction

BRASSEY'S SEA POWER: Naval Vessels,
Weapons Systems and Technology Series,
Volume 1

Brassey's Sea Power:
Naval Vessels, Weapons Systems and Technology Series

General Editor: DR G. TILL, Royal Naval College, Greenwich and Department of
War Studies, King's College, London

This series, consisting of twelve volumes, aims to explore the impact of modern technology on
the size, shape and role of contemporary navies. Using case studies from around the world it
explains the principles of naval operations and the functions of naval vessels, aircraft and
weapons systems. Each volume is written by an acknowledged expert in a clear, easy-to-
understand style and is well illustrated with photographs and diagrams. The series will be
invaluable for naval officers under training and also will be of great interest to young
professionals and naval enthusiasts.

Volume 1 — Modern Sea Power
  DR GEOFFREY TILL

Volume 2 — Ships, Submarines and the Sea
  DR P. J. GATES AND N. M. LYNN

Volume 3 — Surface Ships: An Introduction to Design Principles
  DR P. J. GATES

Volume 4 — Amphibious Warfare
  JAMES D. LADD

Volume 5 — Naval Electronic Warfare
  DR D. G. KIELY

Other series published by Brassey's

Brassey's Battlefield Weapons Systems and Technology Series, 12 Volume Set
General Editor: COLONEL R. G. LEE, OBE

Brassey's Air Power: Aircraft, Weapons Systems and Technology Series, 12 Volume
  Set
General Editor: AIR VICE MARSHAL R. A. MASON, CBE, MA, RAF

For full details of titles in the three series, please contact your local Brassey's/
Pergamon Office

MODERN SEA POWER

An Introduction

by

GEOFFREY TILL
*Royal Naval College, Greenwich and Department of
War Studies, King's College, London*

BRASSEY'S DEFENCE
PUBLISHERS
(a member of the Pergamon Group)

LONDON · OXFORD · WASHINGTON · NEW YORK · BEIJING
FRANKFURT · SÃO PAULO · SYDNEY · TOKYO · TORONTO

U.K. (Editorial) (Orders)	Brassey's Defence Publishers, 24 Gray's Inn Road, London WC1X 8HR Brassey's Defence Publishers, Headington Hill Hall, Oxford OX3 0BW, England
U.S.A. (Editorial) (Orders)	Pergamon-Brassey's International Defense Publishers, 8000 Westpark Drive, Fourth Floor, McLean, Virginia 22102, U.S.A. Pergamon Press, Maxwell House, Fairview Park, Elmsford, New York 10523, U.S.A.
PEOPLE'S REPUBLIC OF CHINA	Pergamon Press, Room 4037, Qianmen Hotel, Beijing, People's Republic of China
FEDERAL REPUBLIC OF GERMANY	Pergamon Press, Hammerweg 6, D-6242 Kronberg, Federal Republic of Germany
BRAZIL	Pergamon Editora, Rua Eça de Queiros, 346, CEP 04011, Paraiso, São Paulo, Brazil
AUSTRALIA	Pergamon-Brassey's Defence Publishers, P.O. Box 544, Potts Point, N.S.W. 2011, Australia
JAPAN	Pergamon Press, 8th Floor, Matsuoka Central Building, 1–7–1 Nishishinjuku, Shinjuku-ku, Tokyo 160, Japan
CANADA	Pergamon Press Canada, Suite No. 271, 253 College Street, Toronto, Ontario, Canada M5T 1R5

Copyright © 1987 Brassey's Defence Publishers Ltd.

First edition 1987

British Library Cataloging in Publication Data
Till, Geoffrey
Modern sea power: an introduction.—
(Brassey's sea power; v. 1).
1. Sea-power
I. Title
359   V163

ISBN 0–08–033623–X (Hardcover)
ISBN 0–08–033622–1 (Flexicover)

Printed in Great Britain by A. Wheaton & Co. Ltd., Exeter

Preface

The aim of this book, the first in a series dedicated to the impact of technology on naval power, is to look at the way the world's navies operate; to see what they take their roles to be and how, broadly, they seek to perform them; and finally to look at how they have adapted to changes in the political, legal and, in particular, the technological environment in which they operate. This volume, then, will concentrate on naval roles: its successors will concentrate on naval means. In this volume, many issues will be raised; in the others, we hope, progress will be made towards resolving them.

I would like to record the very real help given me by the many naval officers with whom I and the other authors of the series have discussed these issues over the past few years. There are too many of them to name individually but I hope that they will accept this general expression of grateful appreciation. My colleagues at Greenwich have been very helpful too, most particularly Professor Peter Nailor and Dr John Pay for their advice both general and particular, John Richards for the illustrations and Kathy Mason for enormous secretarial help. I would also like to thank Commodore Jeremy Blackham and Eric Grove for reading the manuscript and Captain Colin Cameron for his general support. Anthony Watts of the *Navy International* was very helpful indeed in the matter of illustrations. Despite all this help, the responsibility for errors lies with me: I should also emphasise that views expressed in this book should not be taken necessarily to reflect official policy or thinking in the United Kingdom.

Royal Naval College
Greenwich

GEOFFREY TILL

About the Author

Dr Geoffrey Till is Principal Lecturer in the Department of History and International Affairs at the Royal Naval College, Greenwich. He is also a member of the Department of War Studies at King's College, London. He has written a number of books on maritime affairs including *Maritime Strategy and the Nuclear Age* and *The Sea in Soviet Strategy*.

Contents

List of Abbreviations

ACV	Air Cushion Vehicle
ASW	Anti-Submarine Warfare
CG	Guided Missile Cruiser
CIWS	Close-In-Weapon-System
CL	Light Cruiser
CV	Aircraft Carrier
CVBG	Aircraft Carrier Battle Group
DDG	Guided Missile Destroyer
ECCM	Electronic Counter Counter-Measures
ECM	Electronic Counter-Measures
EEZ	Exclusive Economic Zone
ESM	Electronic Support Measures
FAC	Fast Attack Craft
FFG	Guided Missile Frigate
FPB	Fast Patrol Boat
GIUK	Greenland-Iceland-United Kingdom Gap
LPD	Amphibious Assault Transport Dock
LST	Amphibious Vehicle Landing Ship
LSM	Medium Amphibious Assault Landing Ship
MAD	Mutual Assured Destruction
MCM	Mine Counter-Measures
MTB	Motor Torpedo Boat
NATO	North Atlantic Treaty Organisation
NBC	Nuclear/Bacteriological/Chemical
RAF	Royal Air Force
RDSS	Rapidly Deployable Surveillance System
SAM	Surface-to-Air Missile
SES	Surface Effect Ship
SLBM	Submarine Launched Ballistic Missile
SLOCS	Sea Lines of Communication
SOSUS	Sound Surveillance System
SS	Diesel Powered Submarine
SSBN	Nuclear Propelled Ballistic Missile Firing Submarine
SSM	Surface-to-Surface Missile
SSN	Nuclear Propelled Attack Submarine
SURTASS	Surface Ship Towed Away Surveillance System

SWATH   Small-Waterplane-Area Twin Hull
UNCLOS   United Nations Convention on the Law of the Sea
USAF   United States Air Force
USMC   United States Marine Corps
USN   United States Navy
VSTOL   Vertical or Short Take Off Aircraft

List of Figures and Tables

List of Plates

Chapter 8

Chapter 9

1

Introduction to Naval Warfare

NAVIES BEFORE THE BOMB

The Age of Sail

As we shall see later on, many authorities believe that the single biggest technological change that has affected navies in the modern era has been the advent of the nuclear weapon. People can and do argue about the extent to which this is true, but for the moment we will take it as an appropriate point from which to date the modern naval era.

Clearly, the first step in examining the way that navies have changed is to look at what they have changed from. We need in other words to discuss the roles that navies had, and to an extent at least, at how they performed them before the nuclear age. Fortunately we do not have to start from scratch in this because past naval experience has been processed and packaged for us by a whole host of maritime thinkers.

The very first batch of such thinkers in the 18th Century tended to be French and they were concerned above all by the problems of how to turn a collection of sailing ships, subject to all the vagaries of wind, water, rot, heroism, drink and the lash into a coherent instrument of war. Their approach to naval warfare was to try to reduce it to a series of mathematically derived maxims about how forces should be disposed about the naval battlefield so they could achieve their maximum tactical and strategic effect. Their ideas seem largely to be about angles and geometry.

One good example of this is their preoccupation with the fleet commander's getting his force into a line of battle which matches that of the enemy. Doing this meant that the commander stood more chance of being able to control the forces at his command, and also made sure that none of the enemy's ships were left to their own devices. The object of the exercise was then to use the wind and weather to bring a tactically decisive concentration of firepower to bear on a part of the enemy's line.

This diagram shows an ideal way of doing it. It shows a warship approaching the enemy's line at a most carefully judged angle. The point was that the main weapon system of the day was the broadside; this was most effective when fired at an angle of 90 degrees to the line of advance. If a ship could approach as shown in the diagram it could reasonably hope to fire one broadside against enemy warship number 2, and receive in return only a fraction of that ship's broadside, then pass between warship 1 and 2 'raking' no. 1 with a broadside as it did so. In this position it was more or less

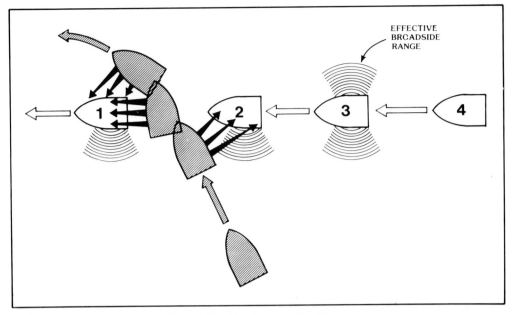

EFFECTIVE
BROADSIDE
RANGE

F$_{IG}$ 1.1 Breaking the Line: The Theory.

safe from the attentions of either hostile warship, but could hope to disable warship 1 so much that it could then turn alongside and finish it off with reasonable immunity. A well trained and handled ship of the line could do all this in three or four minutes.

Something after this style occurred at the Battle of Trafalgar in 1805 when two straight British lines, led by Collingwood and Nelson, speared through the great curving, loosely organised line of the Franco-Spanish fleet. The French and Spanish were spread like a four mile shield between the British and the Spanish coast ten miles behind; opening fire at 1000 yards, the French and Spanish were able to inflict a lot of punishment on the two leading British ships, HM Ships *Royal Sovereign* and *Victory* but were not able to prevent them breaking through the line at two separate points. The *Royal Sovereign* passed under the unprotected stern of the *Santa Ana* and fired a full fifty-gun double shotted ripple broadside at a range of thirty yards which devastated the Spanish flagship. The *Victory* did the same thing against Admiral Villeneuve's flagship the *Bucentaure*. A terrible fire of sixty-eight-pound cannon balls, each accompanied by a keg of 500 musket balls blew in the large gilded windows of the Admiral's quarters in the rear of the ship and raked through its entire length. *Victory* followed this up with another double shotted broadside which killed or disabled one third of *Bucentaure*'s crew. Generally, battles like Trafalgar show two things: firstly, the practicalities of naval warfare in the days of sail were often far removed from the bloodless calculations of naval geometricians; but they also showed that success attended those who best understood and applied the rules that sprang from the technology of the time.

Paradoxically, this most famous of all naval battles came at a time when the technology of naval warfare was on the threshold of a major revolution which rapidly threw all its lessons and implications into the gravest doubt. Within a few

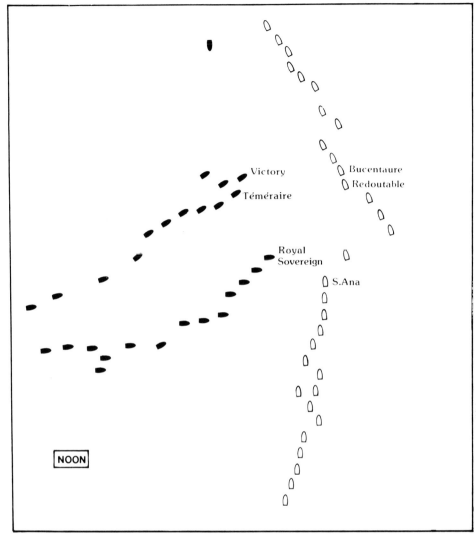

FIG 1.2 Trafalgar at Noon: The British Fleet approaching the enemy line. With the wind coming from behind them, the British ships approach the enemy in two columns.

decades the major naval powers of the world were introducing into their fleets steam propulsion, vessels first clad in iron, then completely constructed from it, breech-loading rifled guns, turrets, explosive shells, mines and a little later torpedoes and submarines.

The Age of the Machine

For the first fifty years or so of the 19th Century, naval thought was almost a contradiction in terms; naval men seemed content largely to parrot the lessons they thought that Trafalgar had taught them. But they gradually began to realise that the

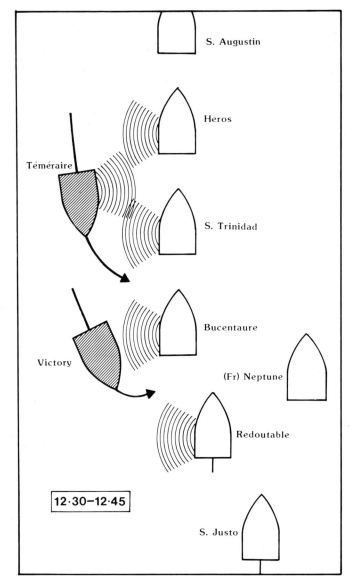

FIG 1.3 Breaking the Line: The Practice. *Victory*, supported by *Téméraire*, about to break through the line
between *Bucentaure* and *Redoutable*.

changes in naval technology brought about by the Industrial Revolution were posing
them with two questions that they would have to answer sooner or later.

The first was the most substantial, and this had to do with the place of navies in
national defence. There were those, even in Britain at the apparent height of its
maritime supremacy, who argued that the advent of steam undermined the traditional roles and even the importance of naval power. After all, they said, if the
French could construct an invasion fleet of steam-driven ships, could they not hope to

take Britain by surprise and rush it over the Channel in a few hours when the British Fleet was port-bound, or away doing something else?

There was, as well, another school of French thinkers prevalent in the last quarter of the 19th Century and known as the *Jeune Ecole*; they argued that battleships were now terribly vulnerable to torpedo-boats and so the naval evolutions that depended on them, such as decisive fleet engagements on the high seas, or blockades, would become too difficult. Indeed a fleet of torpedo-boats could hope to bring even Britain to its knees by attacking its merchant shipping directly.

If all this was true, why should the nations bother with navies of the traditional sort any more? In the fact of these challenges, even Britain's resolution wobbled; the fact that so much of the southern part of the coastline of England is covered with fortifications from Palmerston's days, shows a surprising lack of faith in the Navy's continued ability to defend the country from invasion.

This scepticism was finally epitomised in the last years before the Great War by the British geographer Sir Halford Mackinder who argued that what he called the Columban age, when a handful of maritime powers had dominated the world, was drawing to an irreversible close and that it would be succeeded by the age of the land-powers. Interestingly, technology led the way here too, for it was the advent of the railway and the internal combustion engine, he thought, which would finally allow the land power to develop its potentially superior resources. If this land power was based on what he called the Heartland of the World, that is Central Europe and the eastern part of Russia, the Atlantic powers would find themselves in great difficulty.

The second challenge to naval men was less apocalyptic, but in its way equally worrying. Even assuming that the prophets of maritime doom were wrong, and navies were still as important as ever, how would they conduct their business in the machine age? The tactical conduct of battle would surely be revolutionised by the arrival of steam and the long range gun, but would it be a tightly choreographed affair, fought at a distance, or a confused and vulgar mêlée lost in clouds of smoke? What was to be made of the fact that an Italian battleship had successfully rammed an Austrian one at the Battle of Lissa in 1866? Did this mean that naval men were about to revert to the battle tactics of the age of the galley? The same questions were asked about the attack and the protection of merchant shipping. Were steam driven merchantmen more or less vulnerable now than they were? Should they sail in convoy or on their own? And how would all these technological 'advances' affect the laws of war at sea?

Questions like these had to be answered and were addressed towards the end of the 19th Century by the second batch of naval thinkers, who were this time, mainly of Anglo-Saxon provenance. Foremost amongst them were the celebrated American Admiral Alfred Thayer Mahan (1840–1914) and three Britons Admiral P. H. Colomb (1832–1899), Sir Julian Corbett (1854–1922) and Admiral Sir Herbert Richmond (1873–1946).

People like this countered the sceptics by arguing that sea power conferred so many advantages that countries which possessed it to a significant degree would exercise a dominant influence on the outcome of world events, and with it would come both power and prosperity. Consequently they urged their countries to develop naval power and its civilian maritime corollaries of fishing and merchant fleets, ports, overseas bases and colonies.

Statesmen, and indeed the general public, found these arguments persuasive in the United States and in many European countries too. As a result, international relations from the last quarter of the 19th Century became influenced by naval considerations to a certain extent. Developments like the Anglo-German naval race of 1900–1914 showed that navies could become more than merely an instrument of foreign policy; they could become what foreign policy was actually about.

Of course, the argument was that the sea powers owed their power and prosperity to their likely capacity to prevail in a conflict. The way they were now expected to do this in the machine age was the other great preoccupation of this second set of naval pundits and maritime strategists. Although they all had their individual variations and emphases, their broadly common doctrine was something like this:

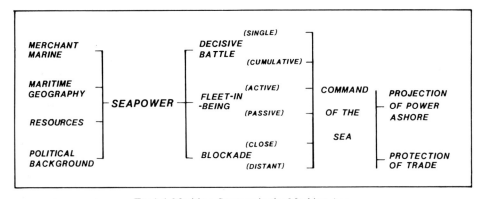

FIG 1.4 Maritime Strategy in the Machine Age.

THE ELEMENTS OF SEA POWER

Broadly speaking, these naval thinkers believed that the degree of sea power which a country possessed reflected how well placed it was in regard to the basic maritime elements. Its *maritime geography* was important, in that it determined the quality of its ports, the shape of its coast, the ease with which it could get out onto the open oceans and concentrate its naval forces into a cohesive whole. The extent to which Russian and Soviet maritime strategy is dominated by geography shows how important such considerations can be.

A *merchant marine* is an important constituent of sea power since its protection provides the Navy with a rationale. Its resources (hulls, sailors and expertise) can buttress naval strength to an important degree. Civilian and naval types of maritime power do not necessarily march together, but the maritime strategists believed that they usually do.

The *resources* affecting sea power depend in large measure on the era in question. In the days when it took five thousand oak trees to make the average man of war, a country's forestry policy in one century could have a significant impact on its naval success in the next. The British re-learned this very necessary lesson in the War of American Independence, when their maritime success was constrained by the arboreal profligacy of an earlier era. Of course, the problems being grappled with by the maritime strategists of the machine age were wholly dominated by the impact of industrialisation on the nature of war at sea. This meant that a country's sea power was directly affected by the state of its economy and in particular by its iron, steel, coal and general scientific capacities.

Finally, there was the important but vague constituent of sea power that derived from the efficiency and sea-mindedness of a country's *government and society*. Some types of these were more conducive to sea power than others; in particular, countries with large and politically important trading communities were likely to be more aware of the importance of sea power than others. On the other han might be more willing to pay for it.

GAINING COMMAND OF THE SEA

—by battle

In a war, each belligerent would seek to incre sea by neutralising the other side's naval forces as much as he could. and obvious means to this end was by physically destroying the a decision or series of battles. Pearl Harbor, Coral Sea and Midway are The Pacific War of 1941–5 has many such instances, for these sea powers which consistently sought battle with each other.

—by maintaining a fleet-in-being

The First World War showed what could happen if one side the other was so weaker that it preferred to avoid the risks of full-scale battle against and to opt instead for some variant of a fleet-in-being order to the German Navy nicely encapsulates

> The Fleet must strike when the circumstances are favourable; it must
> English Fleet only when a state of equality has be by the
> The Fleet must therefore hold back and avoid actions which might lead to heavy losses. This does not, however, prevent favourable opportunities being made use of to damage the enemy.

In effect, the German Navy felt it best to husband its naval resources carefully until such time as circumstances permitted limited forays against sections of the British fleet, or against Britain's more exposed interests. As Scheer pointed out, it was a kind of guerrilla warfare at sea.

In some cases, *both* sides sought to avoid battle with the other. The war between the Soviet and German fleets of the Second War, in the Baltic and the Black Sea, is an example of this. The consequence was an absence of classical engagements at sea between opposing forces intent on each other's destruction, save, that is, for a battle between German armed ferries and Soviet ships and aircraft on Lake Ladoga in August 1942.

—by blockade

Confronted by a weaker power behaving in this manner, the stronger side would usually try to contain or neutralise the weaker by blockade. Blockades might be close, that is off the entrances to the enemy's harbours or distant, where the fleet is simply between the enemy and his possible objectives. The only difference between the two types lay in how much sea room the blockaded party was allowed; in both cases the object of the exercise was to make the enemy's forces an irrelevance but this

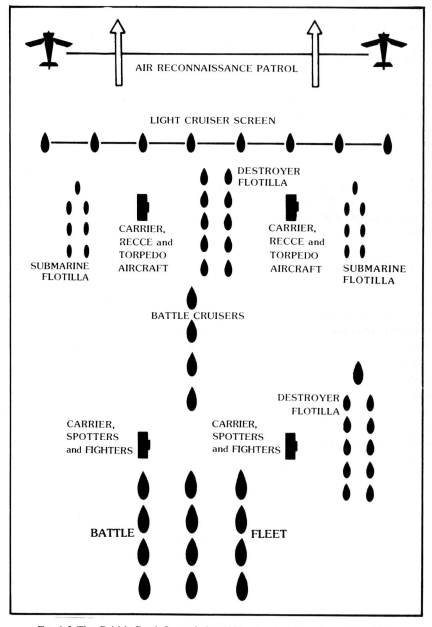

FIG 1.5 The British Battlefleet of the 1920s, in Cruising Disposition. This representation of the Battlefleet illustrates its diversity in the machine age. Its battleships need the support of many different types of warship, submarines and aircraft.

is an arduous and long lasting process. For this reason, strong naval powers usually regard blockade as the less attractive option and try to force battle on the weaker side.

Broadly speaking, the maritime strategists of the machine age argued that by one of these means, and to the extent that it has been successful, a navy can hope to increase, or at least maintain, its capacity to command the sea. The degree of command may vary greatly and is reflected by the extent to which it confers the capacity to use the sea as a means of transportation and as a base from which to project power ashore—all the while being able to prevent the enemy from doing the same thing.

EXPLOITING COMMAND OF THE SEA

The maritime strategists believed that the sea was so important as a means of transportation that operations both to attack and defend shipping were bound to play an important role in any naval war. The Second World War showed them to be right and also demonstrated the extent to which the miltary power of countries like Japan, Britain or the United States depended on the safe and timely arrival of the ships bringing the supplies they needed to prosecute the war.

Moreover, where the antagonists were separated by stretches of water, the sea saw many operations against the shore, ranging from commando raids at one end of the scale to full-scale amphibious assaults like Overlord at the other. Only by this means could a maritime power bring its military capacities to bear against a continental foe. The greater the extent of its capacity to command the sea, the more easily could such a country launch such attacks itself, and prevent its adversary from doing likewise.

Generally speaking, the Second World War, and indeed the First World War too, showed that, despite all the technological advances brought about by the advent of the machine age, the traditional roles and importance of sea power seemed to have survived. Although, in the light of the experience of both wars, the thinking of Mahan and company was refined by more modern writers like Raoul Castex in France, Stephen Roskill in Britain and Bernard Brodie in the United States, the doctrine they put forward seemed to many to have been entirely vindicated.

All the same, the explosion of two atomic bombs over Japan in August 1945 raised many doubts about how much longer this situation would prevail.

2

Politics, Money, Law and Technology

Some authorities argue that, however interesting they may be as explanations of what has happened in the past, the doctrines of the maritime strategists of the machine age do not have much bearing on the activities of contemporary navies. The world, they say, has moved on and things are radically different now. In the next chapter we shall be looking mainly at the way that the technology of war at sea has changed, but before we do, we should consider briefly several other challenges to traditional thinking. These include the possible influence of the changing law of the sea and of various developments in domestic and international politics. But, as we shall see, some of these changes are themselves the result of certain technological developments.

NAVAL ECONOMICS AND DOMESTIC POLITICS

Mahan thought that popular governments were not generally favourable to military expenditure and that, in this respect at least, democratic countries operated at quite a disadvantage compared to those less responsive to public opinion. High levels of military expenditure might threaten the achievement of other national goals in health, education and housing, or worse still, damage the fundamental economic health of the country. This has, of course, always been the case but, according to some analysts, the soaring costs of naval and other weaponry makes the problem a good deal worse now than it has ever been before, even for authoritarian regimes.

Technological sophistication has been an important factor in the burgeoning cost of naval equipment. All defence inflation is higher than ordinary inflation but the rate tends to be worse for navies than it is for armies, because they are more capital intensive. Admittedly, the rate for air forces is even worse, but politically this can be less damaging because the unit costs of an aircraft are much lower than are those for a warship. As a result, navies, when planning their construction programmes, deal with a few quite large blocks of money at any one time. For this reason, those who are seeking to make economies may well be tempted to cut a warship out of the programme because, by this single act, they will be able to make immediate and significant savings.

The problem is aggravated by that fact that technological complexity makes naval planning and constuction a longer and more involved process. As a rule of thumb, it can take up to fifteen years to launch a ship or submarine from the time of its

PLATE 2.1 The 3500 ton Dutch-built *Kortenaer* class of frigate is widely regarded as one of the most successful types to have been produced recently in Europe. (R. Neth. Navy)

inception, although there have been some notable exceptions, such as the Dutch *Kortenaer* class of frigate, where the gap was nearer five years. This lengthy gestation period makes the programme vulnerable to all the many political and economic shifts in government that can take place in that time; moreover, there is a great tendency for the programme designers to amend the programme as it goes along so as to take account of the latest technological developments in hull, weapons or sensors. This process, which the Americans call 'gold-plating', helps make the ship three or four times as expensive as the one it is to replace, and, almost invariably, much more expensive than it was originally thought to be.

Because of all this, the high cost of naval armaments makes them politically controversial, either in terms of where they should be constructed and by whom, or indeed of whether they should be built at all. Faced with these problems, Western governments often feel forced to reduce the size of their fleets.

This has certainly happened in Western Europe where most navies have shown a marked decline in numbers between 1960 and 1976. In very approximate terms, the British fleet has declined by more than 35 per cent in the last decade and a half, the French by 40 per cent, the Dutch by 30 per cent, the Italians by 40 per cent and the Belgians by 50 per cent. They have declined both in terms of number of ships, and in overall tonnage. As a result, NATO Commanders often say they are 50 per cent short in the number of convoy escorts they need and argue that the situation is even worse in regard to maritime patrol aircraft and mine counter measures ships.

TABLE 2.1 *European Navy Size 1960, 1976*

Country	Number of Ships		Tonnage of Ships	
	1960	1976	1960	1976
France	257	155	329,307	318,601
West Germany	127	158	61,881	114,833
Italy	173	103	150,824	133,092
Holland	100	72	140,431	98,846
Belgium	53	28	23,750	9,930
Britain	424	270	662,006	379,173
Canada	60	30	105,617	61,066
Norway	62	94	33,428	31,412
Sweden	199	165	109,808	70,040
Denmark	65	68	21,900	31,252
Iceland	8	7	2,968	6,226
Portugal	61	43	37,953	32,186
Spain	117	101	142,548	119,533
Greece	93	88	78,547	69,552
Turkey	86	183	61,072	98,928

The rate of decline has slowed, however, and there are tendencies the other way as well. Not all Western navies are showing this trend. The increase in the size of the United States Navy under the Reagan administration, for example shows that the reverse may happen too. The Japanese Navy, moreover, may be sustained by only a tiny proportion of that country's GNP, for barely 1 per cent of it is available for the defence budget as a whole. Nonetheless, such is the size of the Japanese GNP that even limited support buys very respectable naval capabilities. According to some experts, the Japanese Navy is about the seventh strongest in the world. Other countries enjoying good levels of economic growth can, at least to some extent, do the same thing. Moreover, even in Western Europe, the position varies to a surprising extent. Several countries, most notably West Germany, Norway and Turkey, have shown an overall increase in the size of their fleets, largely because of the acquisition of coastal defence types of ships.

TABLE 2.2 *European Navy Profiles 1976, 1982*

		Total	Amphibious	Sea control	Coastal defence
France	1976	135	51	64	20
	1982	136	52	57	27
Netherlands	1976	46	11	30	5
	1982	44	10	29	5
Italy	1976	83	31	34	18
	1982	81	28	35	18
Germany	1976	122	22	18	82
	1982	129	28	16	85
Spain	1976	129	19	37	71
	1982	129	21	38	70
Turkey	1976	144	55	26	63
	1982	177	73	27	77
Greece	1976	85	26	32	27
	1982	89	23	30	36
Portugal	1976	77	15	20	42
	1982	63	14	20	29
Belgium	1976	27			27
	1982	31	—	4	27
Norway	1976	83	7	5	71
	1982	86	14	5	67
Denmark	1976	77	—	7	70
	1982	81	—	10	71
Sweden	1976	162	81	25	56
	1982	156	91	14	52

In a more general way, there are some other factors that may partly offset the cost of the new technology. Firstly, it is true that a decline in number is by no means tightly correlated to a decline in capability. Individual warships these days are much more capable than their predecessors in the sense that they can make their presence felt over a much wider area, and more forcefully, than their predecessors could. The power of the modern destroyer when compared to one of Second World War vintage, or the capacities of the *Kirov* when compared to a battlecruiser like the *Scharnhorst*, are obviously worlds apart. The *Scharnhorst*'s nine 11-inch guns could fire about twenty miles. The *Kirov*'s twenty SS-N-19 missiles could deliver a nuclear warhead 250 miles. Of course, this compensating advance in modern capability is cancelled out in a situation where one ship is pitted against another. Moreover, however capable it is, a ship can still only be in one place at a time. So improvements in quality do not necessarily make up for losses in quantity.

Finally, there is a view that the recent trend towards higher naval costs may prove to be no more than a passing phase. Some people argue that technological advances may also make things cheaper. For evidence they point to the impact of the microprocessor, a component whose negligible cost, small size and high capacity makes all sorts of highly capable weapons and sensors economically manageable. In consequence of such advances in micro-electronics, for example, many countries can now afford a fast patrol boat, armed with surface-to-surface missiles, which

PLATE 2.2 The Soviet *Kirov* class of battlecruiser is at 21,500 tons the largest surface warship
to have been built anywhere in the world since 1945, apart from aircraft carriers. (MOD
(Navy))

represents a very respectable naval capacity at reasonable cost. It may well be that
the burden of inflated cost falls more heavily on some tasks, most notably on
'defensive' ones than on others, but we will return to this idea later on.

There are more, certain palliatives which countries under naval cost pressure can
and indeed do adopt to try to make the problem manageable.

—They can consciously explore the possibilities of building cheaper, less
capable ships, maybe with a view to reducing their development costs by
increasing their possible export potential to less demanding Third World navies.
—They can deliberately choose to make the most of the fact that many modern
weapons systems can be packed into an ordinary container and so to speak
'modularised'. This done, the containers can be bolted on to cheap hulls, and
indeed varied as the operational situation demands. Something of the style lay
behind the US Navy's *Arapaho* project for putting aircraft to sea on merchant
ship hulls. Another example of this is the *Meko* frigate produced by Blohm and
Voss in West Germany, where containerised and ready-to-use weapons
systems, command-and-control facilities, and maybe even whole operations
rooms, can be fitted as occasion warrants, with a considerable saving in both
time and money.

PLATE 2.3 The intention behind the Anglo-American *Arapaho* project was to make it possible for the navies of those two countries to deploy VSTOL aircraft and/or helicopters from converted container ships. Ski-jumps could be built over the top of a container-structure, some housing modular units for spares, command and control facilities etc. (Navy International)

—They can just decide to buy foreign equipment. This is often cheaper in the sense that the unit costs are less because of the long production runs that widespread international buying makes possible. On the other hand, most countries prefer to maintain as much productive capacity at home as they can, partly for strategic reasons, and partly because it can offset high defence expenditure by providing jobs and protecting technological expertise, thereby indirectly helping the civilian economy. Although such a policy means higher unit costs (and probably fewer units in service as a result) it does at least mean that the money spent will be largely contained within the national economy. Countries which cannot do this, like Denmark, often argue that this means that naval and military capacity is much more expensive for them than it is for their better placed allies. They are, in a sense, paying over the odds for the same piece of equipment.

—Finally, they can try to collaborate with their allies more, either in the sense of dividing up the tasks more sensibly between them, or of cooperating in the production of naval equipment. The decline in escort numbers, which is largely a function of cost, has given much impetus to the idea of the NATO Standard

Frigate, NFR-90, where eight nation cooperation in the production of a common frigate is expected to lead to substantial cost reductions. The current Tripartite Minehunter Programme under which France, Belgium and the Netherlands have agreed, between them, to build forty-five common minehunters from 1985–1990, shows what can be done in this respect. However, different countries, by virtue of their geography and interests, have different operational requirements and there are often disparities in technological expertise (especially between the United States and its European allies) and hence competing economic interests to contend with. As a result, international collaboration in procurement is often very difficult to organise.

Certainly, despite all the qualifications and palliatives we have noted, the current surge in cost of naval technology poses many countries with actute problems of choice as to what they should build and what roles they should try to perform. In fact, the choice is often a negative one, namely, which capabilities they should give up as being beyond their means. Paradoxically a good deal of this comes about as a result of technological advance.

NAVAL TECHNOLOGY AND INTERNATIONAL POLITICS

Advancing technology has had an important impact on the international context too, and this feeds through into the roles that navies have, and into their behaviour.

Although there have been many wars with a significant naval component since 1945 (the Arab-Israeli wars, the Vietnam and Korean wars, the Indo-Pakistan War of 1971, the Falklands War of 1982, the Gulf War between Iraq and Iran, for example) some restraint in their conduct has often been visible. The belligerents have often refrained from doing things to each other which they could have done. This has been especially true of those conflicts which are related to the main confrontation between East and West, and is particularly noticeable in the case of the Great Powers. As a result, this seems to be a world in which the weak can sometimes bully the strong.

It is not difficult to find examples of this, and some are quite well known such as the Anglo-Icelandic cod wars, or the *Pueblo* incident between the United States and North Korea in 1968. It is also worth pointing out that many of these incidents, such as those between Soviet and Norwegian vessels, challenge the widespread view that it is only Western states that feel the need to practice restraint when dealing with weaker powers.

This kind of restraint would have surprised naval leaders of the time of Palmerston and other naval practitioners of the age of the machine. There seem to be two reasons for it. The first is that the great powers often seem to have been deterred from the full exercises of their naval capacity through fear of the disapproval of 'world opinion', as manifested, for example, by Afro-Asian block voting at the United Nations.

The second reason for restraint is the fear of escalation, whether this is horizontal, where the geographical arena of the conflict widens like ripples in a pool or vertical, where ever more deadly weaponry or practices are introduced into the conflict. In a narrow sense, even the smallest powers of the World can fight with a vigour and an armoury sufficient to make the greatest hesitate. More generally the arrival of weapons of mass destruction, which need not be but most obviously are, nuclear,

PLATE 2.4 One of the West German Navy's 206 class of 450 ton coastal submarines. (FGN)

paradoxically reduces incentives to use force, because the level of destruction could easily outweigh even the benefits of victory.

In this connection, it is often argued, for example, that developments in naval technology, and indeed in naval economics too, have had a certain levelling effect between large and small navies. We have already noted that the ready availability of cheap surface-to-surface missiles and fast patrol boats, such as the Soviet *Osa* and *Komar* classes, might mean that the small powers are stronger vis-a-vis the big ones

PLATE 2.5 Fast patrol boats, like this example of the West German Navy's 380 ton *Albatross* class, are ideal for the defence of inshore waters and when armed with four *Exocet* surface-to-surface missiles represent a significant threat to much larger warships. (FGN)

than they used to be. Indeed, this is the principle behind the whole defence philosophy of countries like Norway, whose Admirals hope to combine the new technology and their own geographic circumstances in a way which will make their waters distinctly unwelcoming to any invading task force, however powerful it may be intrinsically. The advent of sophisticated modern mines, small, silent diesel-powered coastal submarines, shore-based missiles and simple aircraft with air-to-surface missiles may all give the small state more authority in local waters than once it used to have.

Of course, there are countervailing arguments too, as we shall see in more detail later on. Most of these newly potent weapons are those of sea denial, that is they prevent someone else using the sea but do not allow their possessor to use it himself. The strengths they may or may not confer are therefore essentially of negative, not positive, utility. More fundamentally, if the great maritime powers can protect themselves against the much greater threats posed them by their opposite numbers, should they not be sufficient to deal with these lesser threats? And anyway, when we recall the menace posed, in the late 19th Century say, by what were then the new-fangled torpedo, submarine and mine, perhaps we can conclude that the situation today is not, in fact, particularly unusual. Whatever conclusion we come to about this, the proliferation of relatively cheap high technology around a good many of the world's navies does pose some additional problems for the naval planners of the great maritime powers.

It might be that the consequence of all of this is that the political, economic and military costs of using force at sea have risen, perhaps especially for Western states. It may be, therefore, that the value of navies, as a means of protecting or extending the interests of a country, have fallen. As we shall see, others would dispute this view, arguing instead that the new political conditions (which are themselves partly the consequence of technological change) may have altered the way that sea power works, but have not reduced its value.

The Legal Context

The recent past has also been an era in which significant changes have taken place in the way that international law has affected maritime operations. Again, a good deal of this can be attributed to the indirect influence of technology on attitudes to the sea and maritime activities generally.

For example, the demand for marine resources like offshore oil and gas, gravel and manganese nodules in the deep ocean, when added to the more familiar quest for fish, have made the sea more important commercially than ever it has been before. The resultant capital investment has led to a revolution in the technology of fishing and of the exploitation of offshore resources. This, in turn, has made states much more conscious of their maritime rights and opportunities.

It has also led to a widespread recognition of the need to make the law of the sea fit the new economic and technological circumstances. Under the auspices of the United Nations Conference on the Law of the Sea (UNCLOS), a legal consensus has slowly emerged under which the extent of a counry's territorial sea has been extended from three miles (about the range of a cannon shot) to twelve. Fur-thermore, it is generally accepted that, in addition to this, a country should have particular rights in an Exclusive Economic Zone (EEZ) of up to 200 miles from its coastline. There have also been moves to tighten up a country's rights over neighbouring international straits. Finally, there has been some discussion of how the resources of the deep ocean (most notably the manganese nodules), which belong to the whole world community rather than to individual countries, should be equitably exploited.

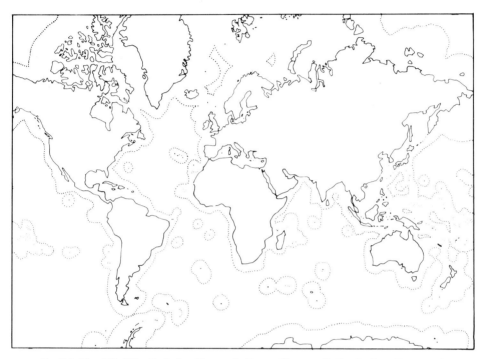

FIG 2.1 The 200 Mile Exclusive Economic Zone. (Source: K Booth, Law Force and Diplomacy at Sea. (London: George Allen and Unwin, 1985))

The traditional maritime states were wary of much of this because they suspected that this enclosure of the open oceans could severely limit their capacity to use the sea in the way to which they had grown accustomed over the past several centuries. They were worried, for example, that a more restrictive legal regime could limit the capacity of warships to sail through the world's hundred or so international straits without let or hindrance. This, in turn, could undermine the flexibility, mobility and general usefulness of their fleets. In the event, UNCLOS agreed on a regime which would guarantee the right of warships to transit such straits in freedom, provided they could do so without threatening the security of neighbouring countries. Although a certain scope for dissension remains, this arrangement has been broadly accepted.

The maritime states were also concerned about some rather more general principles too. For instance, some experts believe that we shall see a natural and growing tendency in nearby states to exert a measure of control over what goes on in their EEZs, again partly in response to the momentum of technological change at sea. This has already happened in many different ways, for example:

—Environmental concerns and anxiety about the effects of pollution on fish stocks has led to measures to extend control over passing oil tankers. Canada has tended to lead the way in this.

—The volume and commercial importance of merchant shipping has persuaded neighbouring countries to seek to regulate it, for example, by introducing traffic separation schemes or by trying to improve their capacity to apply their own laws to merchant ships and their crews.

—The pressure of modern, highly efficient fishing techniques on fish stocks has become so acute, that schemes have been developed to monitor and protect them by such measures as protection of spawning grounds, even if these are in international waters.

While these measures are all quite clearly praiseworthy, they nonetheless add to the misgivings of those who fear that, by just such a process of 'creeping jurisdiction', the EEZs will in course of time become a new and even more extensive territorial sea. This would reduce the amount of 'high seas' very dramatically, and with it might go much of the contemporary value of navies. A glance at a map shows how radical such a change would be. Soviet ships heading for the Atlantic would not be able to reach it without passing through some other country's waters, for example. This explains why the Soviet Union and in fact all the other maritime states are wary about the possible consequences of creeping jurisdiction.

Finally, there is less controversy over what the principles of the law at sea should be, though this is difficult enough, than over how it should be applied. For the moment, at least, the sailors of many countries need fear no loss of their prospects for gainful employment because their countries do not agree with each other about this. The recent Gulf of Sidra incident between the United States and Libya is only the most obvious example of this kind of conflict.

Similar developments have taken place in other areas of maritime law too. Because the UNCLOS section on the sea as a *place d'armes* never sat, there has been little new law enactment on maritime operations as such. All the same there has been a continuing problem in matching evolving technology with existing legislation.

In the past, a warship could demonstrate its 'quiescence', or peaceful intent, by 'letting fly its topsail', training its guns fore and aft with their breeches covered and so on. It is often difficult for a modern warship to show it is quiescent quite so clearly or easily. Does the switching on of a target acquisition radar for a guided missile system constitute a hostile act?

The principle of proportionality has long been an established feature of international law. This says that a response should be proportional to the provocation. But how in an age of missiles and nuclear weapons is this to be managed? In a world of one shot kill weaponry, how can one fire a warning shot across another ship's bows?

Moreover, in such a world, it is hardly surprising that naval men, anxious about the possibly devastating effects on their unarmoured hulls and fragile weapons and sensors of an adversary getting in the first blow, should start to press for the notion of 'anticipatory self-defence', that is the right to pre-empt an enemy who you think is about to hit you.

This has led to the growth of the idea of the 'maritime exclusion zone' where a naval force in time of tension declares that an area of sea around it is prohibited to other ships or aircraft. Accordingly, an intruder will be regarded as hostile and dealt with accordingly. There have been several instances of this kind of thing in recent years, such as in the period before the Falklands campaign, and the current long drawn-out crisis in and around the Gulf.

It is important to distinguish these maritime exclusion zones from those which are simply declared to be firing ranges. Here the object is largely to prevent passing merchant ships from inadvertently straying into danger. But the idea behind the newer type is primarily to help defend a naval force from the kind of surprise attack that modern naval technology makes possible.

All these complexities, brought about largely by the advent of new technology at sea, make naval forces, the sceptics say, less controllable and therefore less useful than they used to be, especially in situations short of all-out conflict. Far from preventing war, such naval forces might in fact provoke it. *Aviation Week & Space Technology* reported an alleged incident during the US Navy's operations in the Gulf of Sidra on March 25th 1986 which illustrates many of the problems brought about by the application of modern technology rather well. It is reproduced here for this reason and not because it is believed to be true!

> The encounter against a ship that was sunk but still not positively identified took place shortly after midnight on March 25. The guided missile cruiser USS *Yorktown* fired two McDonnell Douglas Harpoon surface-to-surface missiles at a contact that had been tracked for some time and came within approximately eleven miles of the cruiser. The Defense Department initially identified the sunk ship as a *La Combattante* patrol boat, but some government officials have expressed concern that the ship with only debris remaining, might not have been Libyan.
>
> 'The *Yorktown* hit what it fired at,' one government official said. 'The intelligence community is investigating the sinking to determine what it was.'
>
> The Defense Department has said that there were four Soviet combatant ships in the area during the US Navy operations in the Gulf of Sidra and the Mediterranean Sea. There was no indication that the ship sunk by the *Yorktown* was Soviet.
>
> *Aviation Week & Space Technology, March 31 1986.*

As we shall see later, it is often said that navies these days are particularly useful in situations of tension, or limited conflict where they can be used carefully as a political instrument to stop a conflict escalating or better still, prevent it from starting in the first place. If technology has indeed increased the danger of sudden attack from close quarters, and has made means of strike more effective than means of identification, as this reported incident would seem to show, the political controllability of naval forces would seem to be compromised. At least this is what the sceptics say!

But, of course, the maritime powers have tried to deal with the legal and political problems brought about by the new technology of warfare at sea. They have sought to control naval activities by much more carefully thought out 'rules of engagement', which take account of the new technology. Also there are agreements like the one between the United States and the Soviet Union of 1972 which was designed to reduce the chances of inadvertent conflict by regulating naval conduct in each other's presence. In effect, the Superpowers decided on a set of rules governing the use of their navies in the new technological circumstances they face, but it is generally agreed that this has 'contained' the problem, rather than comprehensively solved it.

These are understandings about restrictions on the use of naval forces. But the maritime powers have also agreed a need for some control on force levels and force quality lest navies provoke the conflict they are really designed to prevent. For this reason, naval armaments have been included in general arms control agreements like SALT (1972) and have sometimes been the subject of specific treaties like the Sea Bed Treaty of 1971 (which bans the deployment of nuclear weapons on the sea-bed). But it is clear that developing technology means that this is likely to be a continuing problem.

CONCLUSIONS

It is clear that the roles and activities of the world's navies have been affected by a number of developments in the political and legal field. But it is also clear that a good many of these developments have themselves been brought about by the advent of the new technology of naval warfare. We should now move on to look at the direct effects that this new technology has had on naval operations themselves.

3

A Survey of Technological Change

By the end of the Second World War, the established technologies were well developed and their implications well understood. The world's navies had developed quite effective means of defence against both air and submarine attack. Anti-submarine warfare techniques included sophisticated means of signal intelligence, efficient air surveillance from shore- and sea-based aircraft, advanced means of underwater detection based on sonar and a whole battery of anti-submarine weapons, delivered from ships and aircraft. As a result, the German submarine menace in the Atlantic was defeated, although there were indications that with new submarine classes like the experimental Type XVII and the Type XXI electro-submarine, the balance was starting to shift away from the surface ship again.

Thanks largely to improvements, both in protective anti-aircraft gunfire and in the provision of naval air defence fighter cover, developed by the Americans and British, surface forces were able to take care of themselves against shore based air attacks, such as those by Japanese *kamikaze* aircraft, by the end of the war. The consequence was that, while surface fleets might well sustain serious losses, they were still able to perform their traditional functions. Indeed, with the advent of offensive carrier based airpower, and the greatly improved equipment and techniques associated with convoy operations and amphibious warfare, the major fleets were able to exercise a decisive influence on the outcome of the war.

But all this was suddenly cast into doubt in August 1945 by the atomic bombs dropped on Hiroshima and Nagasaki. In fact, as far as Admiral Sergei Gorshkov, Commander-in-Chief of the Soviet Navy from 1956 to 1985, was concerned, 1945 was the beginning of an era of extraordinarily rapid technological change. He believed it marked 'the start of a military-technical revolution which in scope and depth transcended all the reforms and transformations which had previously occured in the armies and fleets of the world.' As a result, the world's navies have been radically transformed.

NUCLEAR WEAPONS

Nuclear weapons themselves of course seemed to imply the biggest changes to the conduct of naval operations. In 1946, atomic tests conducted at Bikini Atoll showed just how terrible might be the destructive effect of atomic weapons on ships. Bursts even thousands of feet away sank or severely damaged warships; further away still, they stripped off the radar and radio antennae, making the survivors militarily useless. Hitherto, this kind of damage required direct or near hits by conventional weaponry, and this in turn had usually required massed attacks, and large numbers of weapons launched, given the standards of accuracy and lethality then achievable. In the light of what Admiral Gorshkov has called 'the atomic shock', many experts concluded from all this that the day of the large surface warship was over, because there seemed to be very little that it could do to protect itself against this new and frightening menace.

But although this was the most obvious naval implication of nuclear weaponry, it was by no means the only one. There were other more general effects too. The arrival in the 1950s of hydrogen weapons considerably reinforced the view that nuclear weapons would make any war between the major powers short, sharp and generally cataclysmic. In this case, it was far from clear what would be the role of the conventional forces, the navy included. Indeed since most observers agreed that the impact of sea power on military operations ashore was invariably slow to take effect (however decisive it might prove to be in the long run), the world's navies were especially vulnerable in this respect. It seemed to many that the war would virtually be over by the time that navies had prepared themselves to fight. This doubt and general scepticism was summed up in the measured tones of the British Defence White Paper of 1957: 'the role of naval forces in total war is somewhat uncertain.' Or, as Admiral Gorshkov put it,

> It turned out unfortunately that we had some very influential 'authorities' who considered that with the appearance of atomic weapons, the Navy had completely lost its value as a branch of the armed forces. According to their views, all of the basic missions in a future war could be fully resolved without the participation of the Navy.

In the United States, this controversy led to the establishment of the US Air Force, a good deal of bitter inter-service dispute and to the cancellation of the US Navy's supercarrier programme in favour of the construction of a bomber fleet armed with the new nuclear weaponry.

In many ways, all this seemed to be the final vindication of those prophets of air power who, in the course of the famous Battleship v Bomb debate that had taken place in many countries during the interwar period, had argued that land-based aircraft could effectively prevent navies from controlling or using the sea to any useful purpose, and that the advent of strategic bombing meant that wars would be too short for what went on at sea to matter very much anyway.

There was a related argument too, made first by those who thought of nuclear weapons as a means of deterrence, rather than of war-fighting. It seemed to them that the consequences of a nuclear war were so obviously appalling that *any* kind of military operation would need to be tightly controlled, lest it inadvertently plunge the world into a nuclear conflagration. So much so, in fact, that traditional naval operations of the type seen in the Second World War would now either be impossible, or would have to be conducted in completely different ways, calculated to reduce the risk of unwanted escalation.

But although all of this seemed to pose rather a substantial challenge to the traditional role and importance of navies, there was another aspect of the case as well, for nuclear weapons themselves soon began to go to sea, just as airpower had in the interwar period. This had two results.

—Firstly, it meant that at least some of the world's navies were given a new set of tasks to perform, many of which were related to the prospect of using the sea as an area from which nuclear weapons could be launched against the shore. According to Admiral Gorshkov, the impact of this on the conduct of land operations, or on their prevention, were so decisive that navies were now much more important than ever they had been before.

—Secondly, the arrival of 'tactical' nuclear weapons in the shape of nuclear depth bombs, torpedoes or missiles might easily transform the way in which navies would conduct themselves at sea. The nuclear depth bomb, for example, might prove to be one way of dealing with that most difficult of targets, a suspected but silent submarine in difficult waters. The use of tactical nuclear weapons might be a method of comprehensively suppressing shore-based airpower. In other words, the arrival of such weapons would transform not just ways of attacking naval targets, but also ways of defending them.

At the very least they would pose the world's admirals with another set of issues to think about. For example, in the Second World War it had been found that the best way a naval force could protect itself from attack was for it to maximise its capacity for mutual support by putting its individual units as close together as possible. But the prospect of nuclear attack makes dispersion seem the more attractive option. So which formation should naval commanders adopt in times of tension or war?

NAVAL MISSILES

In World War II, the main weapons of naval warfare were guns, torpedoes and bombs of various kinds. These weapons were usually not very accurate and so

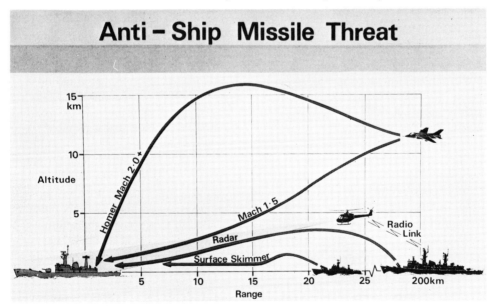

PLATE 3.1 Surface ships are now threatened by a wide variety of naval missiles, launched from aircraft, submarines and other surface ships. Their differing flight profiles require a range of tactical and technical responses. (British Aerospace)

multiple attacks were needed to ensure a hit; they were usually rather short range and so the launching platform, whether it was a ship, aircraft or submarine had to approach its target quite closely, often making it possible for the target to fire back, or indeed to fire first. It was rare moreover for one hit to destroy a ship.

The advent of the naval missile changed all this. In 1967, the Egyptian Navy sank an Israeli destroyer, the *Eliat*, with Russian *Styx* missiles fired from a number of fast patrol boats operating within the safety of Alexandria harbour. Since then there has been considerable improvement in the range, accuracy and lethality of such missiles, whether they are designed to be fired against surface warships, submarines or aircraft. Even relatively short-range anti-ship missiles, like *Exocet* or *Harpoon*, can often allow the attacking platform to fire outside the range of many of the target's defensive systems. This will be even more true of naval cruise missiles like the US Navy's *Tomahawk* or the Soviet Navy's SS-N-19 (which has a range of about 250 miles). The guidance and control systems incorporated into missiles like this (which

PLATE 3.2 The *Harpoon* missile, here fired from a US Navy warship, is a widely used weapon used from and against various naval and air platforms. (McDonnell Douglas)

PLATE 3.3 One hit from an anti-ship missile could easily disable a warship. This shows the effect of one hit by a British *Sea Eagle* missile on HMS *Devonshire* in a recent test-firing. (British Aerospace)

can be fired at and by ships, submarines or aircraft) are such that they can home in on their targets and hit with much higher reliability than used to be the case in World War II.

Of course, the defender's counter to this is to fire his equivalent missiles first, to destroy the attacking platform before it has the time to launch its weapons. There is nothing new about this principle of active defence, for it is, after all, what Nelson did at Trafalgar.

What is new, however, is that the defending platform has a variety of defensive measures it can take *after* the missile has been launched. At this stage it ceases to matter what kind of platform fired the missile. The defender's problem becomes simply one of air defence.

The defender can seek to mislead the incoming missile by a variety of electronic counter measures which are often very sophisticated. The Falklands War showed that the firing of chaff, bundles of metallic strip, into the air often confused the attacker's radars in the same way as it did in World War II. Ships, aircraft and submarines can even be constructed in ways that are designed to reduce their radar signatures. For example, avoiding right angles in their exterior form makes them harder to see.

PLATE 3.4 Metallic Chaff proved to be an effective counter against incoming missiles during the Falklands conflict. Here a 2″ rocket (Chaff Launcher) is being loaded on a Royal Navy frigate. (MOD (Navy))

PLATE 3.5 The *Phalanx* automatic Close-In-Weapon-System is designed to protect a ship against all incoming missiles and aircraft. (General Dynamics)

PLATE 3.6 The Dutch built *Goalkeeper* is one of many European competitors to *Phalanx*.
(Hollandse Signalapparaten B.V.)

All these are technical defences; there are in addition a variety of tactical moves the defender can take to conceal and protect his naval forces, not the least of which is to take advantage of the geographical circumstances in which he finds himself. Submarines can hide beneath ice, can lurk in valleys or holes on the ocean floor, or make the best use of temperature and salinity differences in the water itself to fool the adversary's sonar; moreover they can even hide in the noise areas generated by surface warships. Warships can also try to exploit geography, whether this be by losing themselves in the hugeness of the oceans, or, as in the case of Norway, for example, by hiding in fjords or behind islands.

Needless to say, the incoming missile has developed its answers to these technical and tactical defences too. The trajectory of the missile can be designed to maximise the defender's difficulties in interception, for example, by making it skim just above the surface of the sea at high speed. Moreover, the defender's electronic defences can be overcome by counter counter-measures and so on. In this arcane world, one device is answered by another and the resultant balance between attack and defence constantly shifts.

If the incoming missile cannot be dodged after all, there is a chance of actually shooting it down, possibly with a point air defence missile like the British *Sea Wolf* system, or the advanced and very expensive American *Aegis* system. Finally, there is the possibility of shooting the missile down from the target ship with one of the many rapid firing gun systems currently on offer, such as the American *Phalanx* system. Many of these 'close-in-weapons-systems' (CIWS) as they are known, can fire at a rate of several hundred rounds per minute.

It is certainly true, these days, that the absence of armour plating in modern warships and the extreme fragility of many of their sensors have greatly decreased their capacity to absorb damage. As a result a warship's incentives to try to avoid damage altogether are now much greater than they were. This has led some experts to argue that surface warships have become so much more vulnerable than they used to be that their utility has declined and, moreover, the naval functions that depend on them will also be that much harder to perform. We will return to this topic later.

Finally, however, there is a contrary point to consider as well. Naval missiles can, after all, be fired by surface ships, and so may give them more power than ever before. With its array of anti-ship, anti-submarine and anti-aircraft missiles, a modern warship can dominate thousands of square miles of ocean, and project its

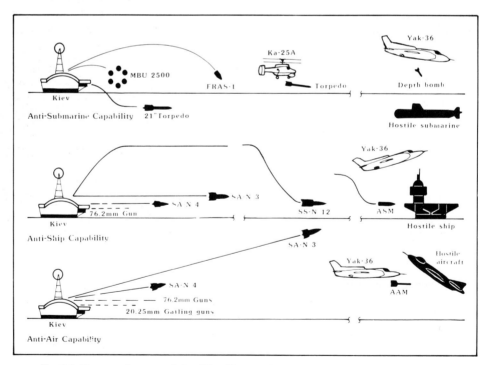

FIG 3.1 Weapons Systems of the *Kiev* (Source: Proceedings of the USNI, US Naval Institute, Maryland, July 1977, p 101)

power far inland too. This diagram of the weapons systems of the Soviet carrier the *Kiev* illustrates the variety of ways in which the modern warship can make its presence felt in the age of the naval missile.

PROPULSION SYSTEMS

Changes in methods of ship propulsion and hull construction have always had an immense impact on the conduct of maritime operations. It is hard to exaggerate the differences brought about in naval warfare, for example, by the transition from the galley to the galleon, or wooden sailing ship to the steam-driven ironclad. Since 1945, the two main developments in this field have been the gas turbine engine and nuclear propulsion systems. Both are advantageous in that they make only modest demands on ship space and manpower.

But the advantages of nuclear propulsion are such that the world's major navies are making more and more use of it. Nuclear propulsion makes fleet operations potentially more independent of the land, endurance being limited largely to the stamina of the crew. Calculations show that nuclear propulsion systems may also prove to be cheaper than conventional systems in the long run.

Needless to say, there are disadvantages too. The avoidance of radiation hazards complicates ship design to an extent and may occasionally hinder surface warships in the conduct of some of their tasks, particularly those peacetime ones which call for ship visits to countries whose governments may be sensitive to nuclear issues.

But the chief beneficiary of nuclear propulsion has been the submarine. By the mid 1950s, the US and Soviet navies had both solved the problems of fitting nuclear propulsion systems into submarines. For a number of reasons, this seems to have increased the submarine's power relative to other naval forces:

—Nuclear propulsion greatly improves the submarine's mobility because it allows higher sustained speeds for reaching distant stations. Needing to be able to range across the Atlantic, and particularly the huge Pacific Ocean, the US Navy has made virtually all its submarines nuclear powered. The driving force behind this policy has been the famous Admiral Rickover.
—Nuclear propulsion allows for a much higher manoeuvring speed in combat.
—Nuclear power allows a submarine to stay submerged for months at a time. For the first time it becomes a true submarine and not just a submersible. A diesel powered submarine must come close to the surface to charge its batteries and can only hope to stay submerged for a day or two at a time. When a submarine rises to the surface, it becomes much more vulnerable to all means of detection and attack, and so this quality of nuclear powered submarines makes them much safer.

For such reasons as these, some experts maintain that nuclear power in submarines has reversed the situation that had been reached at the end of World War II, when anti-submarine forces had largely contained the submarine menace. Nowadays, they suggest, the nuclear submarine makes surface ship operations much more hazardous than they were before. The protection of merchant shipping against submarine attack becomes even more difficult too.

Needless to say, the nuclear powered submarine does have some drawbacks

PLATE 3.7 The Italian Navy has a special interest in hydrofoils. The 59 ton *Nibbio* has a crew of 10, and carries 2 Otomat-Teseo missiles and a 76 mm gun. (CNR Muggiano)

however. It tends to be large and so unsuitable for operations in shallow waters, and the need to keep cooling water pumping around its reactor means that its machinery tends to be noisy, though there have been considerable advances in the business of quietening them in recent years. The modern diesel submarine, on the other hand, presents a smaller sonar and acoustic signature and so can be very difficult indeed to find.

Whatever their means of propulsion however, hydro-dynamics impose certain unavoidable physical limits on conventionally hulled warships, especially when it comes to questions of speed. This explains the current interest in alternative hull-forms (together with the new propulsion systems that normally go with them).

Some of the alternative to conventional mono-hull vessels currently being explored around the world and particularly in the Soviet Union, include the small-waterplane-area twin-hull (SWATH), the power-augmented wing-in-ground-effect PAR-WIG vehicle, surface-effect ships (SESs), air cushion-vehicles (ACVs) and hydrofoils. As Admiral Gorshkov has remarked of developments in his own country,

> The building of ships with dynamic principles of support has already become a reality. There is no doubt that the appearance in large numbers of such ships as part of the fleets will increase their combat possibilities and that the surface forces will be able to solve more successfully combat tasks and acquire new qualities.

PLATE 3.8 The 250 ton *Aist* is the world's largest operational air cushion vehicle, and is in service with the Soviet Navy. Powered by gas turbine engines it is fast and powerful, and has ramps at bow and stern for loading/unloading troops, tanks and armoured personnel carriers. The ACV makes an effective amphibious warfare ship. (Navy International)

PLATE 3.9 ACVs are also useful for minesweeping. Here the British BH-7 is especially fitted for this role. (MOD (Navy))

The Soviet Navy has shown considerable interest in using hovercraft as amphibious warfare ships, for example. In the West, on the other hand, considerations of seaworthiness, expense and endurance have so far limited hovercraft to such coastal roles as mineclearance, but many experts believe there is a great future for such novel types of hull design. If they are right, new ship types like these will offer radically new capacities and demand new operational concepts and tactics. Hull shape and propulsion is so fundamental to naval operations that important changes in this will certainly effect everything else.

OCEAN SURVEILLANCE

Until quite late in the machine age, the single most important thing about the sea which determined the nature of maritime operations was its size. The vastness of the oceans gave some naval forces ample opportunity to hide and others the tremendous task of finding them. It meant that large naval forces were often forced to disperse, and exacerbated the Commander's problem in trying to control them or to wield the fleet as a cohesive unit. Modern means of surveillance and control have helped to transform the situation in the nuclear age.

Let us take the concealment/location problem first. In World War I, Admiral Bacon was only exaggerating a little when he likened the Atlantic to,

> England, and Scotland and Wales rolled flat, all hedges, towns, lakes, rivers removed until it was a sandy waste. One single rabbit in that vast area would be relatively the same in size as a submarine in the North Atlantic. Moreover, it would be a rabbit which could disappear under the sand in half a minute without leaving a track behind it.

This meant that concealment/location was often at the very heart of naval warfare. In World War II, the main surveillance systems were high frequency direction-finders, which picked up radio transmissions, and aircraft, which searched both electronically and by the 'Mark 1 Eyeball'. Signal intelligence, such as the type known as 'Ultra', together with code-breaking systems based on the first electronic computers, considerably helped the protagonists to detect and understand each other's movements. However, this knowledge was at best partial and could be circumvented to a degree by various tactical and technical counter-measures. As a result, concealment/location was arguably the most important element of such campaigns as the pursuit of the battleship *Bismarck* or the fighting of convoy battles in the Atlantic campaign.

Many of these location devices have their updated successors today but new technologies have been added as well. Although there are many such advances, as we shall see in a later volume, three seem particularly important and relate respectively to ships, submarines and aircraft:

   —Firstly, there are long-range radars, infra-red detectors and electronic signal monitoring equipment mounted on satellites which can detect ships on the oceans hundreds of miles below them.
   —Secondly, bottom mounted acoustic arrays like the American SOSUS system can hear passing submarines and pass such information electronically to a central command which can then arrange for more precise location by other means. Much is expected here of sonar arrays which can be towed behind surface ships or submarines.
   —Thirdly, airborne early warning systems like the Boeing E3 A AWACS aircraft, which can detect all manner of flying objects over thousands of square miles.

There is another more general point as well, and this particularly relates to submarine operation and location. The world's knowledge of the oceans, and in particular of the ocean floor, has advanced enormously over the past generation or so. Whatever the motivation behind the Soviet Union's huge hydrographic fleet, for example, superior knowledge of the physical shape of the ocean floor or of polar ice formation could easily be of quite decisive importance to the outcome of any future war. The side which knew the arena of combat better than its adversary would have a tremendous strategic and tactical advantage in the business of concealment and detection.

As a result of such improvements, the movements of aircraft, ships and sub-marines around the world's oceans can be known with more precision than ever before. If the position of the enemy were known with total accuracy, the whole nature of warfare at sea would change. The chances of strategic and tactical surprise would diminish; uncertainty would decline; the role of chance would decrease.

PLATE 3.10 AWACS aircraft should provide the fleet with advanced warning of hostile air activity. Their sophisticated electronic equipment can handle many different aircraft and missile contacts simultaneously up to 250 miles away. With the aid of in-flight refuelling, the endurance of the aircraft is largely governed by that of the crew. (Boeing)

But of course, technology is no more a one way street in this area than it is in any other, for all these advances have their counters. Satellites and early warning aircraft can be fooled or shot down; bottom mounted detection systems are fixed and therefore vulnerable themselves to detection and attack. It is for all these reasons that many experts believe that the critical battle for superiority these days is not in firepower or propulsion systems but in the acquisition and handling of data.

COMMAND AND CONTROL

Data-handling is also critical to the hyper sophisticated command and control systems of modern fleets. This is what Admiral Gorshkov has to say on the matter:

> A most important means of controlling forces and weapons is the communications systems which play a particularly important role in navies since their forces are constantly present in different areas of the oceans, often far from their shores. Therefore, a modern fleet needs global communications capable of ensuring the control of forces many thousands of kilometres away. Moreover, it is necessary to ensure the control of the forces of the fleet operating on water and under water, in the air and on the land. It is not hard to see that the creation of such a communication system represented a problem of enormous scientific and technical complexity. Many countries have worked on this. The task is being solved successfully in our fleet.

Admiral Gorshkov has told us that it will be necessary to wield the scattered units of his fleet, wherever they are on the world ocean and whether they be ships, submarines or aircraft, as integral parts of a cohesive whole which can act and react simultaneously in response to the local situation or to the requirements of Naval High Command in Moscow. Indeed, in its famous *Vesna* exercise of 1975, the Soviet Navy impressed the experts by doing precisely that; all around the world, Soviet forces were suddenly found to be carrying out the same evolutions at exactly the same time. This much enhanced ability to orchestrate the actions of a fleet on a global scale represents a considerable advance on the situation that obtained at the end of World War II.

This improvement is largely the consequence of extraordinary advances in data transmission and handling. These advances include the use of communications satellites, which get ever more sophisticated with each passing year, the exploitation of very low frequency radio, and above all perhaps, the use of computers, both at sea and on land.

Of course, there is another side to this development too. Over the years experts have pointed out several drawbacks of the new technology:

—Once, the flow of information used largely to be from the ships into the central naval authority. Now it could be the other way about. This could limit the operational flexibility and freedom of 'the man on the spot'. Some analysts believe the Soviet Navy to be prone to this kind of over-centralised direction.

—Ships are always more vulnerable when they are trying to communicate with each other or with the central authority. Submarine detection in World War II was greatly helped by the submarine's need to send reports back home. This is as true now as it was then, because means of detecting messages have advanced in parallel with means of sending them.

—Data-handling has not kept up with data transmission. One lesson of recent wars and exercises seems to be that combatants may become deluged by the flow of information. Might not central authority succumb to the temptation to send large amounts of sometimes superfluous information, largely because it has the capacity to do so? This could easily swamp the recipient.

—Worst of all, because the means of communication and control are evidently so important, they will certainly be the object of attack. This could penalise especially those fleets who have come to rely on them too much.

It is not easy to come to any hard-and-fast conclusion about where the advances in communications technology have left the modern navy. Just as one technical development is in some sense 'answered' by another, so are the advantages at least partly offset by disadvantages.

ELECTRONIC WARFARE

Over the past ten to fifteen years, it has become increasingly clear that the microchip has also revolutionised naval operations by making possible considerable advances in the area of electronic warfare. The extent to which this has become true was made plain, really for the first time in the Arab-Israeli War of 1973, and confirmed by the Falklands conflict of 1982. Before this, people tended to concentrate their attention on 'hard-kill' weapons which actually blew up ships or sank submarines because the importance of their development was obvious. But these more recent wars showed that the less tangible parts of the naval armoury were becoming more and more important, and the world's navies have now started to procure electronic warfare systems in a major way.

These systems would include the enormous range of naval radars and sonars, both to detect hostile ships, submarines and aircraft, and to get 'fire control solutions' on them. These systems are backed up, or supported, by Electronic Support Measures (ESM) which might for instance facilitate the reception and analysis of radar signals, and put them into a kind of order of anticipated threat. The satellite intelligence effort is a particularly important part of a major navy's electronic order of battle these days.

Electronic Counter Measures (ECM), are intended to defend the ship, submarine or aircraft from such surveillance as this by various means of electronic deception, including jamming, the use of chaff and the sending of false or misleading signals to decoy enemy forces away.

Needless to say, there are counters to ECM too, or Electronic Counter Counter-Measures, (ECCM). In fact, the arcane world of electronic warfare shows particularly well the way in which advances in one area of military-technological development tend to be answered by corresponding advances in other areas. Because Electronic Warfare is such a new and vital part of naval warfare, we will be devoting a good deal of attention to it later in this series.

The whole issue of technological change in war at sea constantly throws up a number of such complex but important issues. Some of these will be examined in the next chapter.

4

The Implications of Technology

This chapter will introduce some general issues which new technology raises for naval professionals involved in the design and operation of naval forces. They will be introduced here very briefly, but will crop up again later in this book when the modern functions of navies are addressed in more detail. They will also be found to recur in the subsequent volumes in this series concerned with specific naval weapon systems.

TECHNOLOGY: QUALITY AND QUANTITY

Technology raises many real problems of balance for naval planners, and for others concerned with the optimum size and shape of navies, to solve. In the first place, what balance should be struck between the high-capability ships needed for the most demanding tasks and the more modest ones capable of dealing with lesser commitments?

In the early 1970s, Admiral Elmo Zumwalt was the US Navy's Chief of Naval Operations and he came to believe that because of the pressure of vested interests, the Navy had got out of balance. There was too much emphasis on platforms and weapons being of the very highest quality: this meant that they were very expensive and so tended to be few in number. While quality was important in dealing with a very capable adversary, numbers mattered too. Moreover, there were many other tasks (like the naval presence role, convoy escort and so forth) which called above all for large numbers of hulls in the water. For this reason, he decided that the US Navy needed a new 'Hi/Lo mix' as it came to be known, with relatively more emphasis on the Lo part of the equation.

Accordingly, the drive to produce glamorous and expensive ships like large strike carriers was muted by a greater attention being paid to the idea of less capable less expensive 'Sea Control Ships' that would have been rather like the British *Invincible* class. At the same time, more resources were devoted to mundane ships concerned with the support of amphibious warfare or the ocean escort of shipping.

Since that time, the pendulum has swung some way back towards quality in the US Navy, but it is clear that this act of balancing between the alternatives is a constant one for naval planners. In most of the world's navies, it boils down to weighing up the relative advantages of having two good frigates as opposed to four reasonable corvettes. Although the problem is one that is largely set by the pressures of technology and cost, the answers depend at least as much on political and strategic considerations about what the functions of the navy are supposed to be in the first place.

We will conclude this brief review by identifying the kind of arguments commonly deployed by protagonists of both persuasions:

For Quality and Against Numbers

—There are many situations where only the best available will do. A 1 per cent a month engine failure rate may be acceptable for London buses, but not airliners, because there is such a difference in the consequences. A submarine will probably only get one chance to sink a surface target, so its torpedoes must be as effective as possible.

—A ship capable of dealing with the worst threat is also capable of dealing with all lesser ones. It is therefore more flexible and more capable of coping with the unexpected. This is important because many of the situations in which naval forces find themselves are unpredicted, and often essentially unpredictable.

—During the Battle of the Atlantic in World War II, both sides made every endeavour to stay ahead in the technology race, and the advantage went first one

PLATE 4.1 The Royal Fleet Auxiliary *Reliant* was originally the merchant ship *Astronomer* and was converted for war use during the Falklands campaign. In 1983 it was refitted, partly as a trials ship for the *Arapaho* containerised aircraft support system. (British Aerospace)

way and then the other. If either had abandoned this effort, it would have been technologically outflanked by the opposition, and almost certainly defeated.

For Numbers and Against Quality

—High quality means high cost which means fewer ships. However good they are, ships can only be in one place at one time, so the fewer the ships, the less the coverage.

—Humdrum ships (like converted merchant ships) are often surprisingly good 'force multipliers' because they provide more decks for helicopter operation, confuse the enemy by producing more blips on his screens, increase the force's capacity to sustain losses, and so on.

PLATE 4.2 RFA *Reliant* is shown here in San Carlos Waters, Falkland Islands, alongside the Merchant Vessel *Scottish Eagle* on charter to the British Ministry of Defence as a refuelling unit for Naval vessels. Auxiliary ships of this sort are indispensable 'force multipliers'.
(MOD (Navy))

—The more technologically sophisticated a ship is, the higher the maintenance task, and the 'down time'. Simple, robust equipment is usually far more reliable, and in war, reliability matters a great deal.

—Better technology can often be defeated by better tactics anyway. Thus, in the Battle of the Atlantic, U-boats countered ASDIC by simply sailing on the surface, although by so doing they did expose themselves to other threats.

Needless to say, all these arguments are open to challenge, for the debate is one that is truly never-ending in professional naval circles. There are moreover, no permanent and complete answers to these questions. Any solution arrived at will tend to be the compromise between the two persuasions that best suits the particular case—and, of course, the cases can be very different.

TECHNOLOGY AND MANPOWER

The relationship between technology and manpower is a more complex one than may appear on the surface. A glance at the defence budgets of the developed countries shows that manpower costs (training, salaries, conditions of service, pensions, etc) have grown to an enormous extent relative to other areas of expenditure. There are often hidden costs too. Modern ship designers, for example, have to work to much higher standards of habitability than they used to, in the form

PLATE 4.3 Accommodation is an important element in modern warship design, because of its impact on crew endurance and personnel retention. Larger ships and submarines, like the French SSBN, pictured here, can usually meet these demands better than smaller ones. On the other hand, their deployments are usually longer too. (French Navy)

of cubic feet per man, general crew facilities and so forth. This often causes real problems in getting other features into the ship such as engines, weapons and sensors that the naval staff might want. Western ship designers, in fact, are sometimes accused of making their ships *too* comfortable in that they make too little provision for armament, as compared with, say, the Russians.

In addition there is often a great deal of difficulty in getting the necessary manpower at all. The technological and managerial demands of modern navies require just those qualities in their personnel which are so much in demand (and therefore often so much more highly paid!) in the civilian economy. This is not just a problem for capitalists either. Shortages are reported in the Soviet Navy of particular groups of skilled men, such as nuclear engineers, and this is not just a function of the expansion of that navy.

But it is probably the Third World which has the worst manning problems of all. Starting a navy requires a big effort in the provision and training of crews for the ships themselves and of manpower for the supporting infrastructure, but the cost in terms of the loss of skilled people to fragile developing Third World economies is often severe. Skilled people are an even scarcer and more valuable resource in the Third World than they are elsewhere.

PLATE 4.4 The Operations Room of the British ASW carrier *Invincible* shows how technologically demanding modern naval operations can be for personnel of all levels. (MOD (Navy))

For understandable political reasons, such navies also often try to diversify their sources of supply in naval equipment. As a result of this, they get a mix of equipment which may not work together particularly well. This reduces the prospects of economy of scale in the acquisition of equipment and considerably complicates the maintenance task.

Given all these problems, it is not surprising that the idea of reducing manpower has considerable attractions for naval planners, and one way of doing this is to encourage automation. Automation can lead to the same kind of substantial reduction in the number of men required to operate ships and submarines as it does the size of the workforce in car factories.

A glance at some aspects of West German naval experience shows that considerable progress has been made in this direction already. For instance, the 1936 German destroyer *Karl Galster*, 2400 tons displacement, had a crew of 313; its modern equivalent would be the 2400 ton frigate *Augsburg* whose crew is only 200. A less direct comparison also produces essentially the same result for if we divide the displacement of the Second World War light cruiser *Emden* by the crew number, we get a figure of 8.8 tons displacement per man; doing the same sum for the modern guided missile destroyer *Hamburg* produces a figure of 11.9. In short, both methods show a reduction of about one third in the manpower needed to operate large surface ships . . . in the West German Navy at least!

If this trend is projected forwards, the result would be completely automated weapons and platforms, rather a radical way of solving the manpower problem! The

PLATE 4.5 The 2400 ton West German frigate *Augsburg*. (FGN)

PLATE 4.6 The 3340 ton West German destroyer *Hamburg*. (FGN)

PLATE 4.7 The *Seehund* is one of three unmanned warships used in the West German *Troika*
minesweeping system – a portent of things to come? (FGN)

existence of such automated systems as the Vulcan/Phalanx close-in-weapon-system, and the unmanned ships of the German *Troika* minesweeping system show that this possibility is not entirely theoretical.

However, in practical terms, the trend in manpower reduction is most unlikely to continue at the same rate. There seems to be an irreducible minimum in crew numbers, which is partly a function of the manpower demands of a range of unavoidable operational and maintenance tasks (eg 'fighting the ship', replacing faulty equipment, damage limitation and so on). For the foreseeable future, the man will remain part of the loop. It may well be that in some types of platform we may already have reached the bottom of the curve. In the German case, for example, the man/ton ratio for modern submarines and conventional minesweepers is not significantly different from what it was in World War II.

There is finally a good deal to be said for the argument that while modern technology may make reductions possible in the number of people required actually to operate the ship, it tends to increase the need for training and maintenance personnel both on board and ashore. One way of reducing the maintenance requirement is to try for a 'maintain by replacement' system but this can be tremendously expensive in terms of both capital investment and storage space and so is not usually regarded as a general solution to the problem.

In short the relationship between technology and manpower is nothing like as simple as may appear at first glance. It is an important general issue for naval planners, and those interested in their problems, to keep in mind.

TECHNOLOGY: OFFENCE AND DEFENCE

The issue of whether emerging technology aids the defence more than the offence, or the reverse, is so large that we will do no more than raise it here. It will be found constantly to recur later in this book and in this series as a whole.

But one aspect of the matter should be identified clearly even at this stage, and that is the view that the relationship between the defence and the offence is profoundly different at sea to what it is on land. On land the intrinsic advantages of defence (greater opportunities for concealment, knowing the ground, closer proximity to base areas and so on) are usually held to be so great as to require the attacker to have a three to one numerical superiority in order to be reasonably certain of winning. Of course, it is easy to think of exceptions (such as the Arab-Israeli wars, where the smaller side won) but this is nevertheless the generally accepted rule of thumb.

But at sea, the ratio often seems to be quite different and, if anything, the other way around, giving all the advantages to the offence. If we take, for example, Admiral Gorshkov's figures for the battle of the Atlantic in the Second World War, the difference becomes clear. According to him the Allies had to deploy against the German submarine force over thirty aircraft carriers, 3500 convoy and other escorts, and 1500 landbased aircraft. 'To every one German submarine,' he says, 'there were twenty-five ships of the Allies and a hundred planes'. While we may quarrel with his exact figures, there can be little doubt that in the battle of the Atlantic, as in most other naval campaigns, the natural advantage lay with the offence, rather than the defence. As we shall see later, sea denial is easier than sea control, and the real point to bear in mind is whether new technology makes this better or worse.

TECHNOLOGY AND THE MANAGEMENT OF CHANGE

The huge range of technological changes that have affected navies since 1945 means that naval planners have to be able to react sensibly to an enormous range of problems, and the management of such change is even more difficult now than it used to be. It not only requires the exact understanding of the technological present but also involves making judgements about the technological future. Admiral Gorshkov puts it like this:

> Until recently, the scientific method of managing the building of the fleet was based on the analysis of the current possibilities of science and technology and their development in the near future. Now, into this sphere has come scientific forecasting based on estimated lines of weapon development, electronic technology, power, shipbuilding theory and a number of non-military sciences, the state of which influences the development of a fleet.

It is, he says, all very complicated. The point is that the necessary process of continuous adaptation to an uncertain and changing future is fundamentally a problem of management policy.

The way a navy reacts to this challenge depends in large measure on the circumstances in which it finds itself. Most obviously it will reflect the kind of navy it is. Perhaps four basic kinds can be discerned:

1 *The Global Navy* will be able to deploy significant forces around the world's oceans simultaneously. Probably it will have organic airpower of some sort, amphibious capacity, and distant water sustainability and can fight against sophisticated opposition for long periods of time. Requiring huge expenditure in defence resources, this category is effectively limited to the navies of the Superpowers.

2 *The Bluewater Navy*, to a certain extent, can do the same thing but has less resources and therefore a much more limited capacity to conduct distant operations simultaneously, especially if against sophisticated opposition. The navies of Britain and France come into this category since they can, and do, operate regularly in waters far removed from their shores.

3 *The Regional Navy* needs to be strong in its own local seas. This is a very broad category into which a large proportion of the world's navies fall. To be able to exert an influence significantly beyond its own shores, the regional navy will need a number of major surface warships and modern submarines at least. Such navies will often have a modern amphibious capacity as well. Into this category would come such navies as those of India, Japan, West Germany, the Netherlands, Italy, Brazil, Argentina and so forth.

4 *The Coastal Navy* is the largest category of all. It comprises most Third World Navies, and many of the more modest European ones. The thrust of their policy is to do their best to protect coastal waters against all comers, and will be characterised by a concentration on fast patrol boats, mine warfare vessels, and perhaps coastal submarines. The range is wide and covers everything from the limited coastguard navies of the Third World to the quite sophisticated standards of the Swedish Navy, for example.

These categories are only very rough and ready of course, but they do at least suggest that different sorts of navies have different sorts of problems in managing technological change. The bluewater and regional types in fact may find their problems particularly difficult. The global navies have the resources to back many of the runners in the race, and their need to cover a wide range of capabilities wins general political acceptance at home. The coastal navy, on the other hand, does not have the luxury of choice and is resigned to modesty. It is the bluewater and regional navies who have the real problem, for as France's Admiral Moineville has remarked:

> In point of fact, many countries are in an intermediate situation where they certainly cannot be prepared for all events but where they have all the same, enough resources to have options to choose from. It is for these nations, then, that the problems are greatest. The most obvious mistake is to define the naval forces of such a state as a scaled down version of a very large navy, since the smaller navy is almost bound to lack both political purpose and technical coherence.

Typical Errors

All the same, the historical record suggests that navies are not especially good at managing technological change however large or small they may be. When he watched the battlecruiser *Queen Mary* blow up during the Battle of Jutland in May 1916, Admiral Beatty is reported to have remarked: 'There seems to be something wrong with our bloody ships today.' He repeated the remark the following day,

PLATE 4.8 The loss of the British battlecruiser *Queen Mary* during the Battle of Jutland in 1916. (Imperial War Museum)

adding significantly, '. . . and something wrong with our system too.' Historians have identified four main areas of deficiency:

1. There have been errors of *policy*, in working out how technological developments have affected priorities between the various tasks that navies need to perform. In World War I, for instance, the advent of the submarine should have increased the importance of assigning destroyers to trade protection, relative to screening duties with the Grand Fleet. The British Admiralty were slow to recognise this, however.

2. The failure to appreciate the importance of the submarine was in itself an error in *weapons procurement*. This failure to appreciate the significance of such technological advances as the advent of steam, or the torpedo, or naval aviation, is often held to be the consequence of naval traditions of conservatism. Occasionally though, it may be the other way around, with a tendency to over-react to technological advance. When ASDIC arrived, for example, there was a widespread tendency to think that it had solved the submarine problem.

3. In cases of *operational* error, the results of the new technology were not used or countered properly, such as the very tardy introduction of convoy-and-escort as an answer to the submarine in World War I.

4. There have also been errors in *personnel management*, that is the matching of people to technology. It is often said, for example, that during the interwar period, the best officers were positively dissuaded from entering such new and risky technology-based branches of the naval profession as aviation.

Some historians go down one level and try to deduce what the underlying faults that led to these four categories of error actually were. Their suggestions are many:

—Decision-making failures in adapting to the new technology are often said to be the result of the comparatively short tenure of most naval office-holders. Does their constant coming-and-going not make it difficult to generate a long-term consistency of purpose, In the interwar period. Admiral William Moffett ran US naval aviation for thirteen years; after the war, Admiral Rickover dominated the US navy's nuclear propulsion programme for decades; Admiral Sergei Gorshkov commanded the Soviet Navy from 1956 to 1985. In all cases, arguably, the benefits easily outweighed the costs.

—Good decision-making depends on the efficient transmission of information up and down the hierarchy but the habits of deference associated with naval discipline may make this difficult.

—Navies are large organisations and naturally tend to develop bureaucracies with standard operating procedures which may not allow them to adapt to new technology effectively. Bureaucratic inertia may easily slow down or distort the proper introduction of new equipment.

Military men, it is sometimes argued, have loyalties which make it difficult to foster a scientific habit of thought. Writing of the interwar period, Basil Liddell Hart complained of the perverse adherence that the Admirals of his day had to battle-ships. He wrote:

> 'I also came to realise that to most Admirals the respective value of battleships and aircraft was not basically a technological issue, but more in the nature of a spiritual issue. They cherished the Battlefleet with religious fervour, as an article of belief defying all scientific examination.'

Professor Blackett writing of the introduction of Operational Research, which eventually transformed the way that technology was used in the conduct of the anti-submarine campaign in World War II, frequently complained of the military men's apparent preference for fighting the war on the basis of 'gusts of emotion' rather than on scientific analysis of the results so far attained, especially if these findings seemed to conflict with common sense. The long resistance to the idea of introducing large convoys, because it seemed to put all the eggs into one basket, is a good case in point.

This may easily spill over into a profound scepticism about the boffins and other progressives who offer unpalatable advice. The memoirs of scientists involved with military men during World Wars I and II are full of references to the deep suspicions they so often seemed to generate in their colleagues' minds.

PLATE 4.9 These *Orion* class battleships exemplify conventional concepts of the Battlefleet in 1917 and for the next twenty years too. (Imperial War Museum)

A Case for the Defence?

Of course counter arguments to much of this can be put. First, the facts of naval conservatism can be challenged. While some historians may criticise a navy for excessive caution in the introduction of some new technology, others may, and in fact do, congratulate it for its far-sightedness. In truth, a good many experts have complained about the miltary being *over keen* on new technologies, a characteristic leading to the tendency to 'gold-plate' ships and submarines already remarked upon.

There is also the point that a dash of conservatism is often a good thing anyway. It is often said, for example, that in the introduction of a new technology there is a kind of S curve at work. For a long while there is a period of steady but unspectacular progress; then there is a period of spectacular advance; finally, progress slows into no more than a rising plateau of incremental development. Since, in the period of steep advance, a particular weapon or ship may easily be built today but rendered obsolete tomorrow, heavy investment may be most unwise at that stage, and a wait-and-see policy much more sensible.

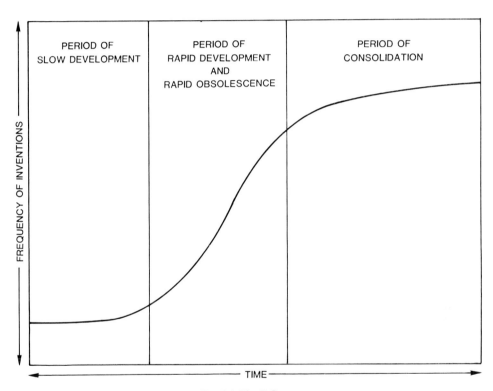

Fig 4.1 The S Curve.

Hindsight allows historians to distinguish the road from the technological cul-de-sac much more easily than contemporaries could possibly have done. For every technical advance that works there are many many more which do not. The Royal Navy's continued interest in 'submersible battleships' during the interwar period is an example of a concept that seemed very attractive at the time but proved crazy in the end. It is therefore only natural that military men should be on their guard against such chimaera.

Finally, some countries have more incentives to innovate than others. For example, Britain's pre-eminence in wooden sailing ships meant it was other countries that had the more compelling reasons to investigate new types of warship, and bear the heavy research and development costs of the pioneer. Britain had the industrial capacity to overhaul the pace-setter later, more or less when it chose. The Royal Navy adopted this wait-and-see posture as a deliberate policy. As one contemporary commentator, Sir George Clark, put it: 'It should be an axiom of our policy never to lead in ship construction but always to follow with something better.' The British only abandoned this arguably very sensible policy when the industrial lead which made it possible slipped away from them. The laying down of the world's first all-big-gun battleship, HMS *Dreadnought* in 1904 was an early example of the alternative policy which, at first sight, might seem to suggest more technological open-mindedness, but which in fact sprang largely from Britain's changed circumstances.

Conclusions

So what conclusions should be drawn from this brief review of the problems that navies have in managing new technology?

Complexity of the task

The first obvious lesson, is that they *do* have a problem; the swirl of new technology is getting more diverse and the rate of significant innovation is getting faster. Moreover, the new technology is itself affected by a variety of political, strategic and economic circumstances which complicate the situation still further. The complexity of the naval planner's task is finally aggravated by the fact that different types of technology develop at different rates, and there is always an acute problem in reconciling them.

For instance, it may take up to fifteen years to move from the conception of a new project like a major warship to the construction of the first unit in the series. Moreover the operational life of the warship's hull may easily prove to be twenty-five years or, in some cases, even longer, because the rate of technological innovation here is not as fast as it is elsewhere. But the speed at which technological developments in such related fields as weapons, sensors and communications are likely to come over that period of forty years, means that the planner has not only to be able to forecast the future (a notoriously difficult business) but also to marry up the consequences of technical advance in a large number of different areas.

Finally, the naval planner has, fortunately, only very limited opportunities to test out his products in war. However sophisticated forecasting and decision-making aids like systems analysis and conflict simulation may be, and however determinedly navies try out their skills in exercises, the experience of combat invariably throws new light on the matter.

The Problems of Navies

The second lesson to be drawn from all this is that navies are themselves large organisations and have the same kind of management problems that all large organisations do. But they also have extra ones that derive from their military character, such as the short tenure of many of their office-holders, difficulty in quantifying output and productivity, institutionalised deference, the officer's preference for being on the bridge of a ship at sea rather than behind a desk in the Ministry, and so on.

Although the extent to which navies react inappropriately to the advent of new technology is a matter of debate, and in fact varies widely from navy to navy and from time to time, it can hardly be doubted that there is room for improvement. In the 19th Century, technical advance played an important part in professionalising navies; it encouraged a proper career structure and increased the need for effective staff work and staff training. The situation would seem to be the same now. The challenge of contemporary technology is such that the world's navies will need to continue their own reform if they are to keep up with their own technology. And once again that reform will doubtless be largely in the area of training, education, staff work and decision-making where the demands of the computer age are at their most acute.

TECHNOLOGY AND NAVAL ROLES

The technological revolution of the 19th Century produced a batch of naval thinkers anxious to explore its implications for maritime strategy and operations. The advances of the nuclear age have done exactly the same thing. In the United States, for example, Admirals Elmo Zumwalt and Stansfield Turner have both written widely on this topic. Admiral Turner's characterisation of the modern functions of navies looks like this:

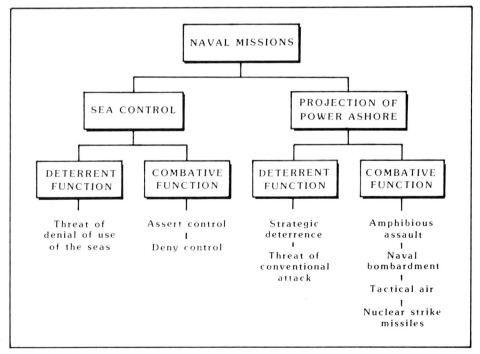

FIG. 4.2 Maritime Strategy: An American View. (Source: Jonathan Alford (Ed)), Sea Power and Influence: Old Issues and New Challenges (The Adelphi Library no. 2), International Institute for Strategic Studies, Gower Publishing, Farnborough, 1980, p. 66.

Broadly, he divides the wartime functions of navies into two large and comprehensive missions, namely Sea Control and Power Projection and the peacetime ones into the Strategic Deterrence and Naval Presence missions. This stress on the peacetime functions of navies is relatively new, and did not figure much in the writings of the naval thinkers of the machine age. No doubt this is partly in reaction to new technology, especially the nuclear variety, which promises to make warfare potentially even more horrific now than it used to be in the past and which has therefore tended to focus attention on various methods of war prevention, rather than simply on war fighting.

A great many other naval thinkers have put pen to paper on the impact of the new technology on the conduct of maritime operations, many of them reflecting the circumstances of the nation they are most concerned with. France's Admiral Hubert Moineville with his 'Naval Warfare Today and Tomorrow' is a particularly thoughtful example of the genre. All the same, and perhaps rather unexpectedly, pride of place must surely be given here to the Soviet Union's Admiral Sergei Gorshkov, Commander-in-Chief of the Soviet Navy from 1956 to 1986, whose book 'The Sea Power of the State' (first published in 1976 in Moscow but with an English language version and a second edition in 1979) is certainly one of the most extensive analyses of the subject to appear since 1945. For a supposedly secretive society, the Soviet Union's Admirals are surprisingly candid about the missions and methods of its navy, although there are problems and pitfalls in interpreting what they have to say about it. Broadly, Gorshkov's categorisation of the missions of the Soviet Navy looks something like this:

WAR TASKS	FLEET v FLEET	1 SEA DOMINANCE 2 HOMELAND DEFENCE 3 STRATEGIC DEFENCE
	FLEET v SHORE	4 STRATEGIC STRIKE 5 OPS v SHORE 6 MARITIME INTERDICTION
PEACE TASKS		7 GENERAL DETERRENCE 8 NAVAL DIPLOMACY 9 LIMITED & LOCAL WAR

FIG 4.3 Missions of the Soviet Navy.

It will be seen from this that Soviet writers tend to divide the wartime tasks of the fleet into two categories, namely fleet versus fleet and fleet versus shore. Because wars are usually fought about land, and fundamentally decided upon it, Soviet writers tend to argue that the second category is basically more important than the first. Nevertheless, Sea dominance is generally regarded as the prerequisite for the remaining five war roles. Generally, Soviet writers distinguish less sharply between war roles and peace roles than do their Western counterparts. One of the reasons for this is that the capacity to succeed in peace will follow the perceived capacity to succeed in war.

Conclusions of the New Thinkers

Briefly, the new analysts of sea power in the nuclear age have come to two sets of conclusions:

1. While many of the traditional roles of navies, as expounded by the thinkers of the machine age, have no doubt survived largely intact, the many and diverse advances of technology have changed the way in which these traditional tasks are performed often rather considerably. In some cases the change has been so great as to make the advice offered by the traditionalists not only irrelevant, but arguably wrong. In other cases, not only the role, but even the manner in which it is carried out, have changed surprisingly little. Generalisation is difficult; each case needs to be examined specifically.
2. The new technology has produced new roles for the world's navies to perform. Perhaps, in some cases, early versions of the role can in fact be discerned in naval activity before 1945, but their prominence is so much greater now that the role is effectively a new one. In other cases, the technology is so new, that the role associated with it is novel almost by definition. Most modern naval thinkers think there are broadly three 'new' missions for modern navies to perform, namely:
    —*Strategic Deterrence* is the ability to use the sea as an area from which to launch nuclear attacks on the enemy's homeland, a function which is supposed to have an important deterrent function in peacetime. Contained within this mission are actions in general support and the negative ones of trying to interfere with the enemy's ability to do the same thing.
    —*Naval Diplomacy* is a mission which comprises all the ways in which naval power can be used in peacetime as a means of forwarding the interests of the state. It includes everything from courtesy visits and cocktail parties to limited military action of various kinds.
    —*Coastal Tasks* comprise all the many maritime activities associated with the supervision of a country's coastal waters, and their defence against all

manner of intrusions. Given the relative rise in economic value of these waters, this task has become steadily more important in recent years.

In the next few chapters, we will explore the impact of technology on the conduct of all these naval missions, both traditional and novel.

5

Sea Control

DEFINITIONS

Sea control is one of the most difficult, but at the same time one of the most important concepts of maritime strategy. Put very briefly, to have sea control means to be in a position where one can use the sea for one's own purposes, and at the same time prevent an enemy from using it for his. Sea control, in other words, affords freedom of action to those who possess it but denies it to those who do not.

It is a relative quantity rather than an absolute one. A navy will have it to a greater or lesser degree. It is not an absolute which the navy has or does not have. The more one side has it relative to another, the more it can use the sea for its purposes and prevent the enemy from doing likewise.

In many ways it is similar to the concept which the strategists of the machine age called the Command of the Sea, but says Admiral Stansfield Turner,

> This change in terminology may seem minor but it is a deliberate attempt to acknowledge the limitations on ocean control brought about by the development of the submarine and the airplane . . . The new term 'Sea Control' is intended to connote more realistic control in limited areas and for limited periods of time. It is conceivable today to temporarily exert air, submarine and surface control in an area while moving ships into position to project power ashore or to resupply overseas forces. It is no longer conceivable, except in the most limited sense, to totally deny them to an enemy.

In fact, many would argue that navies, even in the good old days, could very rarely, if ever, hope 'to totally control the seas for one's own use or to totally deny them to an enemy'. The difference between the present situation as portrayed by Admiral Stansfield Turner and the previous one described by classical maritime strategists like Mahan and Corbett is merely a matter of degree. New technology need not imply that established theories, concepts or procedures have suddenly become obsolete. Suggestions that the situation is all different now often seem to imply a failure properly to understand what it was like 'then'.

Before we move on from the matter of definitions, it is as well to note the appearance of a kind of negative version of the concept often known as 'sea denial'. Here the objective is not to use the sea oneself, but to prevent the enemy from doing so. It is often said that this was the rather limited aspiration of the Soviet Fleet in the 1950s, a period when the main preoccupation of Soviet Admirals was to prevent their American counterparts from using the waters to the North of the Soviet Union as an area from which to launch nuclear attacks against Soviet territory with their carrier-borne aircraft.

Some experts believe that new naval technology in the shape of 'smart' mines, shore-based guided missiles, aircraft, fast attack craft and small modern diesel submarines are particularly well suited to such modest, even negative aspirations. Also as has been argued above, systems like these are often relatively cheap.

This is often taken to mean two things:

> —Denying the sea has become relatively easier than keeping or holding it, a factor which may narrow the gap between small sea-denial navies and large sea-control ones.
> —Some ways of using the sea require forms of sea control which call for naval forces to stay at sea in contested and hazardous areas for quite long periods of time. The conduct of amphibious operations would seem to come into this category. If smart technology really has made sea denial relatively easier, then this type of sea control, and the naval activities that depend on it, could both have become much more difficult. This in turn could have profound strategic consequences for countries who rely on the use of the sea for positive, rather than merely negative purposes.

The distinction between positive sea control and negative sea denial is also important in that they make different demands on technology. It is often said that sea denial requires a capacity to do damage (with disposable ships of perhaps limited endurance, fire and forget missiles and the tactics of hit-and-run); sea control, on the

PLATE 5.1 A Soviet-built *Osa* Fast Attack Craft in the service of the Egyptian Navy. The acquisition of such craft may be narrowing the gap between the larger and smaller navies, especially if they are equipped with modern SSM. (MOD (Navy))

other hand, requires the capacity for the force, if not the ship, to absorb damage as well as inflict it, possibly over quite extended periods of time, and far out at sea. If the technology for each is different, and this is a matter of dispute, then naval planners will need to have clear ideas of their strategic requirements in sea control/denial before deciding the hardware they want.

SEA CONTROL: METHODS

Admiral Stansfield Turner maintains that there are basically four methods of sea control. They are:

1.   *Sortie Control* This is basically what the strategists of the machine age called blockade, that is of trying to bottle an opponent up in his ports and bases. The idea was then as now to neutralise the enemy's naval forces by preventing either his fleet as whole, or the individual units composing it from getting to sea. Because an opponent has all the advantages of operating from his home base he will probably, these days, have air superiority. This means that 'sortie control tactics' will probably largely depend on submarines and mines.

A good example of this occurred during the Falklands campaign of 1982. The sinking of the Argentine cruiser the *General Belgrano* by the British submarine HMS *Conqueror* had the effect of confining the surface units of the Argentine Navy, which were quite considerable, to an area twelve miles from the Argentine coastline. This made the British conduct of the rest of the campaign much easier.

Admiral Stansfield Turner points out, however, that sortie control is not without difficulties and disadvantages:

—On land it is possible to 'blockade' aircraft, by building static belts of air defence radars and missiles and by maintaining large numbers of air bases with interceptors at high states of readiness. Such defensive systems can be seen in Europe and the Middle East. The environment and the impermanent presence of surface ships makes all this much more difficult to do at sea. For this reason, maritime air blockade may well require bombing the enemy's air bases, often a hazardous and difficult exercise.

—Blockades have never been completely successful. Some units will probably be at sea when sortie control tactics are initiated, and will need to be hunted down. The more responsible the blockaded country was for starting the war in the first place, the more could this be true. Also, historical experience suggests a resourceful adversary will develop methods of wriggling through blockades, to some extent at least.

—Blockades are exhausting, demand the presence of naval forces that could otherwise be elsewhere doing other things, tend to leave the initiative to the enemy and take time to have strategic effect.

2.   *Chokepoint Control* allows the enemy more sea room because it involves the blockading forces falling back to establish their blockading lines across some geographic narrows through which the enemy must pass to reach the open sea. The most obvious example of this is the relative importance ascribed by NATO to containing Soviet naval forces north of a line from Greenland, through

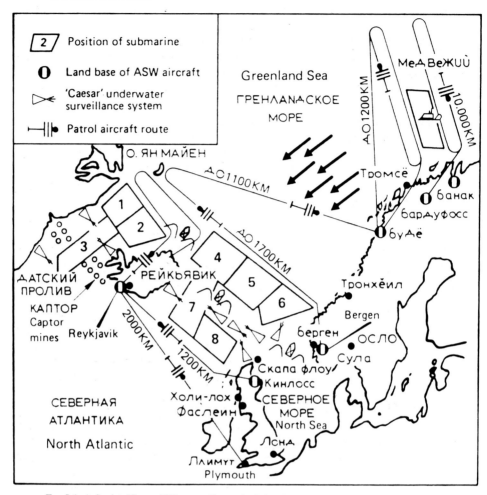

Fig 5.1 A Soviet View of Western Control of the Choke Points to the North Atlantic.
(Source: *Morskoi Sbornik* November 1976)

Iceland to the United Kingdom, the so-called GIUK Gap. Any Soviet forces, be they aircraft, submarines or surface ships, attempting to reach the North Atlantic would need to run the gauntlet of bottom-mounted sensors and mines, and patrols by NATO aircraft, submarines and surface ships operated in this relatively confined area.

Chokepoint control in some ways is similar to the distant blockade imposed by the British on Germany in both World Wars, though being so much further from Soviet territory, it is a looser variant of the concept. It shares some of the disadvantages of sortie control operations, but is less demanding to operate, especially from the air point of view. On the other hand, it leaves the enemy with a good deal more operational freedom.

Most importantly, chokepoint control tactics do nothing about hostile forces that are already out on the open ocean, or who manage to wriggle through blockading lines, except of course to promise to prevent them from returning home.

3.   *Open Ocean Operations* are the first of two sea control methods designed to meet the requirement of dealing with hostile forces on the high seas. It involves hunting these forces down and destroying them. The sheer size of the world's oceans means that the emphasis here is on surveillance and search systems, particularly on aircraft and satellites with their high search rates. Time and patience, Admiral Stansfield Turner warns us, will be required.

It is certainly true that in the past these operations have often resembled looking for a needle in a haystack. For examples of the problem it is necessary to look no further than Admiral Nelson's pursuit of Admiral Villeneuve in the Trafalgar Campaign, or of the exhausting British hunt for German pocket battleships and surface raiders at the beginning of World War II.

However, many experts contend that the huge advances made by surveillance systems noted above have greatly reduced this problem. Since it is so much more difficult to hide at sea now than it was, naval technology has had a particularly important consequence in making open ocean operations relatively easier than they used to be and so more attractive when compared to other methods of sea control.

This is a controversial matter, however. Other experts maintain that advances in deception have kept pace with advances in location, and the resultant situation may not be so different now from what it used to be. Indeed, as far as looking for submarines is concerned, it may be even worse. In consequence, open ocean operations may be no more attractive an option now than in the past.

4.   *Local Engagement* puts the emphasis on *exercising* sea control, say by using the sea to transport supplies, or to mount amphibious operations, and only defending that use if the enemy should seek to contest it. To do this, the enemy's aircraft, ships, and/or submarines must approach to weapons release range of the units to be protected. This of course makes the task of locating hostile forces much easier than hunting them in the open ocean would be. It facilitates the concentration of defensive assets where their presence really matters, and means that hostile forces in other areas of the sea, which are doing no particular harm, can be safely ignored for the time being.

The defending forces in question may be any combination of aircraft, surface ships or submarines whose task will be to destroy hostile launching platforms before they can launch their weapons and/or deflect or destroy the attacking weapons themselves. To Admiral Stansfield Turner this method of sea control '. . . amounts to positioning forces in a limited region and then preying upon the enemy'.

Advocates of this particular method of sea control are at pains to refute the view that this is merely a defensive operation which offers little prospect of actually winning the war at sea, but instead concentrates merely on avoiding losing it. For evidence, they point to the undoubted success of convoy-and-escort in World War II when compared to other methods of sinking submarines. The 1944 Battle of the Philippine Sea, in which the United States naval carrier task force commander simply allowed the Japanese to launch one air strike after

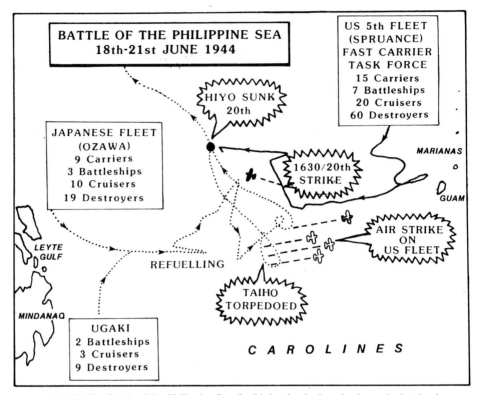

FIG 5.2 The Battle of the Philippine Sea. In this battle, the last classic carrier battle of
World War II, Admiral Spruance practised defensive tactics and shot down over 300
Japanese strike aircraft in what became known as the 'Great Marianas Turkey Shoot'.
This phase of the battle was followed by a more 'offensive' one in which 1 Japanese
carrier was sunk and another damaged.

another at his forces, and shot all the aircraft down when they arrived, is another
example of the genre.

On a somewhat more philosophical note, they also argue that sea control, in
any case, is no more than a means to an end, and if the sea can be used to
strategic effect without first of all winning sea control, then so much the better.
Why waste time and effort in hunting down hostile naval forces which are not in
contention, and which cannot prevent 'the defender' from using the sea to help
win the war?

Critics of the defensive-offence method of sea control remain unconvinced,
however. They deploy several arguments:

(i)   This method of sea control assumes that the defender will be able to
       contain the enemy's first attack, by dealing with either his launching
       platforms, or the weapons he launches, and will then be able to go onto
       the attack. But many analysts believe that evolving technology aids the
       offence more than the defence and this would cast doubt on the wisdom
       of the tactic.

(ii)   It allows the enemy greater capacity to decide the time, place and nature of the battle. By definition, therefore, the battle will take place on terms more favourable to him than would have been the case if the defender were establishing them.

(iii) The defender's capacity to prosecute the 'offensive' part of the battle may easily be compromised by his simultaneous need to defend the merchant shipping or amphibious forces in his care.

(v) Local engagement does nothing about hostile naval forces elsewhere. It leaves the initiative to the enemy and does not attack his interests directly.

For all these reasons, more offensively-minded naval analysts suggest a fifth alternative method of securing sea control which Admiral Stansfield Turner does not describe directly. This alternative has recently come to be known as Forward Operations.

5.   *Forward Operations* are not however a new idea. They are simply the latest variant of a mode of naval thinking that was, for example, exemplified by the English fleet's successful attempt to defend the shores of England against the menace of the Spanish Armada by attacking Cadiz in 1587. The British fleet's attempt to lure the German High Sea Fleet out to its destruction in the early part of World War I by trailing its coat across the southern part of the North Sea was a more general example of the concept. The Japanese attack on Pearl Harbor illustrated the same desire to 'take the fight to the enemy'. There are many such examples of this type of thing.

The common idea behind them is that forward operations are the best way of keeping and exploiting the iniative, because it allows the force conducting them much more latitude to decide the time, place and nature of the combat than would be the cases were he simply responding to attacks from the enemy.

This kind of thinking has recently been well exemplified by Admiral Thomas B. Hayward, then Chief of Naval Operations of the US Navy:

> We must fight on the terms which are most advantageous to us. This would require taking the war to the enemy's naval forces with the objective of achieving the earliest possible destruction of his capability to interfere with our use of the sea areas essential to the support of our overseas forces and allies. In this sense, sea control is an offensive rather than a defensive function. The prompt destruction of opposing naval forces is the most economical and effective means to assure control of the sea areas required for successful prosecution of the war and support of the US and allied war economies. Our current offensive naval capabilities centred on the carrier battle forces and their supporting units are well-suited for the execution of this strategy.

What the advocates of such a strategy for the US Navy appear to have in mind is a whole range of naval activities. They are at pains to refute the common view that all they are suggesting is for, say, a Carrier Battle Group to sail up the Kola fjord and flatten Murmansk. Instead, a whole spectrum of forward activities would be involved including offensive mining of the enemy's ports and anchorages, a range of submarine activities against the enemy fleet, and surface actions of various types.

The advantages of such a strategy in the United States and NATO case are that it would prevent the Soviet Union from deciding the rules of the game and deploying its forces to its own best advantage. Its advocates believe, for example, that this is NATO's best way of defending its long and vulnerable sea lines of communication in new technological circumstances which generally

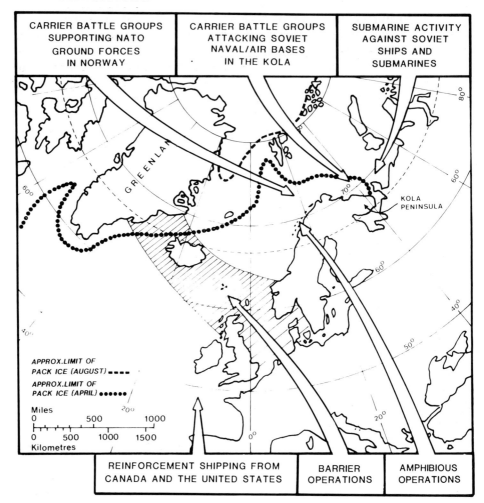

| CARRIER BATTLE GROUPS SUPPORTING NATO GROUND FORCES IN NORWAY | CARRIER BATTLE GROUPS ATTACKING SOVIET NAVAL/AIR BASES IN THE KOLA | SUBMARINE ACTIVITY AGAINST SOVIET SHIPS AND SUBMARINES |

| REINFORCEMENT SHIPPING FROM CANADA AND THE UNITED STATES | BARRIER OPERATIONS | AMPHIBIOUS OPERATIONS |

FIG 5.3 US Navy: Forward Operations. In addition to the conduct of barrier operations across the GIUK gap and the support of reinforcement shipping coming across the Atlantic, the US Navy currently would expect to operate extensively in the waters off Northern Norway.

favour the attacker. More specifically, NATO is in a worse position than were the Western Allies of World War II, because they have limited defensive assets, a much more severe potential submarine threat, fewer merchant hulls to use, and less time to get their forces and supplies across to Europe. Instead of relying on passive convoy-and-escort, the argument concludes, Western navies should go for a forward strategy of manoeuvre, initiative and offence.

Methods of Sea Control: Conclusions

Two conclusions emerge from this survey of Admiral Stansfield Turner's four methods of securing sea control and the fifth alternative which currently has some prominence in the US Navy.

First and most obviously, these are matters of argument and controversy and much of the debate comes from differing views of the nature and the implications of the latest technology of war at sea. Judgements about specifically technological issues do much to determine judgements about the best sea control tactics and strategy to adopt. But these technological issues, some of which will be reviewed shortly, are essentially unresolved and do much to account for current uncertainties.

Secondly, abiding uncertainties reinforce the historic tendency not to go just for one of these alternatives, but for a mix of many, or even of all, of them. Few serious advocates of any single alternative would pursue it to the point of completely excluding the rest.

THE INSTRUMENTS OF SEA CONTROL

After describing what were the main methods of sea control, Admiral Stansfield Turner then identified what he thought were the main instruments by which it would be contested. His conclusions are summed up in this diagram:

TABLE 5.1 *Weapons Systems Appropriate For Sea Control*

Weapons systems	Tactics:	Sortie control	Chokepoint control	Open area operations	Local defense
Submarines		X	X	X	X
ASW aircraft			X	X	X
Fighter aircraft			X		X
Surveillance systems		X	X	X	X
Attack aircraft		X	X		
Mines		X	X		
Escort ships		X	X	X	X

Source: United States Naval Institute, *To Use the Sea*, Naval Institute Press, Annapolis, Maryland, 1975, p. 9.

If he had included forward operations in his list of sea control tactics, he would no doubt have maintained that they would require the full set of weapons systems, just as do chokepoint control operations. The diagram shows the advantages of what maritime strategists call the balanced fleet, since the greater the variety of weapons systems available, the wider the range of operational possibilities. A properly balanced mixture of maritime weapons systems, they say, increases naval flexibility, and the capacity to respond to changing or unexpected circumstances.

In effect, a balanced fleet offers navies the kind of all-round capacity that makes it difficult for their adversary to outflank them either by tactical or technical means. Admiral Gorshkov is also quite clear on the matter. He says that the Soviet Union needs the:

'Harmonious balanced development of the force of the ocean-going navy matching the demands of the time, capable of opposing any strategems of foes and of confronting an aggressor with the need to solve himself the very problems which he is creating for our country.'

Such a range of capacities requires a judicious mix of surface ships, submarines and aircraft. Nevertheless the precise nature of the mix is the subject of intense debate in the world's navies. Moreover, the optimum mix may be affected not only by the set of tasks the navy in question thinks it needs to be able to perform, but also by technological changes. To explore this idea, we will look in turn at three different types of weapons platforms, which are usually regarded as being valuable for various types of sea control operations, namely submarines, aircraft carriers and surface warships. How has technology effected them, and their relative place and import- ance in the hierarchy of tasks concerned with the contesting of sea control?

Submarines

Most analysts agree that the power of the submarine has increased in an absolute sense even if we exclude the rather special type designed to fire ballistic missiles, which will be considered later. Some of the technological reasons for this have already been mentioned in passing but it will be useful to repeat them here, and add a few more:

—*Propulsion systems* Nuclear propulsion systems, as we have seen, increase the submarine's capacity to hide because it no longer needs to rise towards the surface to recharge its batteries. Moreover nuclear propelled submarines are faster both tactically and strategically; they can move to the battle area, and around it, much more quickly than submarines with more conventional forms of propulsion. All this greatly increases their fighting power vis-a-vis the surface ship. On the other hand, the need to keep cooling water pumping around the reactor makes them easier to hear. They also tend to be physically large, which makes them unsuitable for operations in shallow waters.

It would be wrong however, to conclude that diesel powered submarines are, by

PLATE 5.2 Fleet submarines are now usually bigger than most surface ships. Here the 4000 ton submarine HMSM *Courageous* sails in company with the 2450 ton frigate *Penelope*. (MOD (Navy))

PLATE 5.3 At 455 tons the West German 205 class is, in comparison, a much smaller coastal
submarine of a type often difficult to detect. (FGN)

comparison, useless. Modern smaller variants, like the German 209 type, are small
and therefore particularly well suited for operations in shallow water. They are often
very quiet, and so difficult for surface forces, or indeed other submarines, to find.

—*Constructional features* also may increase the relative power of the submarine.
The Soviet Navy, for example, has made the *Alpha* class of submarine out of
titanium; this is extremely expensive and constructionally very difficult to do. But the
resultant hull strength means that the submarine can dive to depths which make it
very difficult to get at. Furthermore, the material itself has a low magnetic signature
and so is more difficult to detect. Anechoic coatings on the outside of submarines
absorb noise generated from within the submarine and so make it more difficult to
hear and also absorb sonar signals from outside; the 'quieting' of machinery proceeds
apace as well. All this will make the submarine more difficult to find, although at least
partially compensating advances in detection systems may be expected as well.

Finally, the shape of submarines, and even what they are painted with, makes
modern nuclear and diesel propelled submarines relatively faster than they used to
be. Since 1945 the speed and endurance ratio between submarine and surface ship
has moved considerably to the latter's disadvantage, a factor which has a considerable bearing on their relative fighting power.

—*Electronics* have been transformed by the replacement of solid state com-
ponents by the microchip and the micro-processor. The smaller size of the resultant
equipment in submarines saves space, which can be used either for more spares
(which increases endurance) or for more weapon and sensor systems (which

increases fighting power). Submarine sensors have also benefitted considerably from the new electronics, with the result that targets can now be acquired at far greater range than they used to be. In the past, a submarine's capacity to find a target was limited by the range of its optical periscope. The operational records of World War II are full of reports of German U-boats going to sea and failing to locate a single target in their Atlantic patrols. The modern improvements in a submarine's sensors have therefore considerably increased its power in relation to all forms of surface ship.

PLATE 5.4 The 3700 ton *Alpha* submarine of the Soviet Navy. The *Alpha* is large, armed with torpedoes and anti-submarine missiles, made out of titanium alloys and nuclear propelled. (MOD (Navy))

—*Submarine Weaponry* has also advanced in three main areas. Torpedoes are now much smarter than they used to be and can be fired to good effect against other submarines, and surface ships at ranges in excess of 15 nautical miles. Even while submerged, submarines can fire cruise and other naval missiles against other submarines, surface ships, land targets and even air targets, the accuracy of all of which is much enhanced by targetting information generated from within the submarine itself, or from other maritime platforms including satellites. Lastly, modern submarines can launch highly intelligent mines. These improvements on the technology that existed at the close of World War II have profoundly changed the relationship that once prevailed between submarine and surface ship.

Although as we shall see later on, anti-submarine devices of various types have also improved considerably in the past several decades, it is generally agreed that technology has resulted in a net improvement in the relative position of the

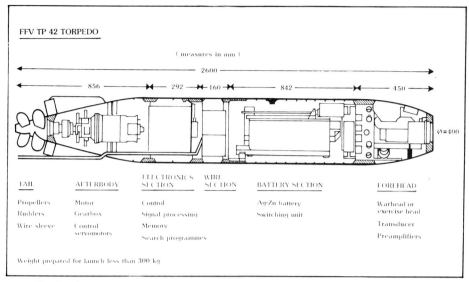

FIG 5.4 Construction of the FFV TP 42 Torpedo. This company specialises in producing lightweight air-dropped or submarine-fired torpedoes which are wire-guided but which also automatically home in on their targets. (Source FFV, Sweden)

submarine, when compared to other maritime platforms like aircraft, surface ships and aircraft.

The operational significance of this is not easy to summarise. On the one hand, submarine related technology has opened up new fields of maritime strategy, particularly with regard to the deployment, prosecution and protection of those submarines expressly intended to fire nuclear or conventional missiles against the shore. For the first time, submarines can intervene directly in the land battle, possibly with quite decisive effect.

On the other hand, they can perform more familiar tasks with greater effectiveness. Their ability to participate in the battle for sea control is now much enhanced,

PLATE 5.5 The *Stingray* torpedo can be launched from helicopters, maritime patrol aircraft and surface ships. (Marconi)

and really for the first time the old dream of a 'fleet submarine' has been realised. Moreover, the threat they pose to merchant and military shipping has dramatically increased.

In all these ways, the modern submarine has become a major actor in all aspects of naval warfare. It is now no longer simply a weapon of sea denial, but fundamentally one of sea control and sea use, and much more important in relation to other weapons of sea control than it used to be.

Aircraft and Aircraft Carriers

The news that the Soviet Navy has at last built a 'proper' aircraft carrier, after maintaining for years that these were no more than floating incinerators is a useful contemporary reminder of the fact that nowadays, navies cannot function without air support. The general consensus is that serious sea control aspirations require both land- and sea-based aircraft. The latter may include helicopters operated from surface ships, mini-carriers such as the British *Invincible* class or the Italian *Garibaldi*, or fleet carriers such as the awesome *Nimitz* class of the US Navy.

The role of aircraft carriers in naval operations has been a matter of acute controversy from the closing stages of World War I when they made their operational debut. In the nuclear age, changing technology has meant that this is still very much the case. The debate concentrates on three issues, all of which have an important bearing on the part played by aircraft and aircraft carriers in sea control.

(i)   *Economic costs.* The high cost of aircraft carriers is a function of the size of the hull and the sophistication of the aircraft carried. Because it should be able to deal with air, land, sea surface and underwater adversaries simultaneously, a fleet carrier needs to have aircraft for ASW, reconnaissance, air combat, air strike and electronic warfare; these aircraft can easily weigh from twenty to forty tonnes and their operation in sufficient numbers and in all weathers demands a good deal of supportive equipment, stores and a very large platform. In fact, the bigger the carrier, the more aircraft it can carry per ton of displacement. For such reasons, the aircraft carrier is often said to be a perfect example of the benefits of the economy of scale. But it is also true that in an absolute sense, the bigger the carrier the more expensive it is!

Its aircraft are expensive for the same reasons that all aircraft are, but they suffer two extra disadvantages. First, the special conditions for operating them on board ship impose difficulties in their design. Secondly, the number of carrier aircraft operated, ordered and built is typically smaller than for equivalent land-based aircraft. For both reasons, their unit costs tend to be higher.

The consequence of all this is that the increasing sophistication of the first line fleet carrier designed for sea control operations means it costs more and more money. Even in the United States, there was a sizeable body of opinion which argued that the costs were too great to be borne and who advocated alternative solutions, such as the mini-carrier concept developed in Europe. Generally though, it was argued that fleet carriers were essential for sea control operations outside the range of friendly air cover, and highly desirable even within it. Since the United States needed to be able to control the sea, it would have to have fleet carriers, however expensive they were. For other countries, the fleet carrier was

PLATE 5.6 The British *Illustrious* ASW carrier of some 20,000 tons. The ship carries a number of *Sea King* Mk 5 for ASW operations. For defence against air attack *Illustrious* carries, in addition to its *Sea Harriers*, *Sea Dart* missiles, visible just forward of the flight deck, two *Phalanx* CIWS (1 forward and 1 aft) and two 20 mm BMARC guns. To keep the ship and her aircraft operational *Illustrious* carries some 60,000 items in her storerooms.
(MOD (Navy))

PLATE 5.7 The Ski-jump fitted to the flight deck much improved the endurance of the *Sea Harrier*. This one is fitted to *Hermes*. The clutter of modern sea/air warfare is visible on the right. (MOD (Navy))

PLATE 5.8 The American *Nimitz* is a nuclear powered aircraft carrier of some 81,600 tons standard displacement. About one third of its mixed airgroup is visible on deck. (US Navy)

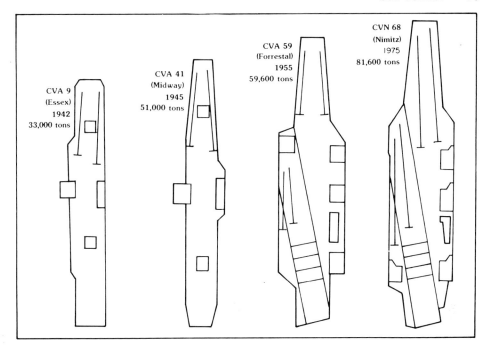

FIG 5.5 Growth in Size of the US Navy's Attack Carriers.

simply not a serious option; cheaper expedients and reduced sea control aspirations were therefore adopted. Even such adulterated versions of the aircraft carrier are beyond the means of most countries, however.

(ii)   *Vulnerability*. The large size of a fleet carrier may increase its power in various ways but it is also a source of vulnerability. Such a vessel is easier to locate and presents a bigger target, then a conventional surface warship. The carrier's high cost and its operational prominence in most ambitious sea control activities make it a desirable target for an adversary to attack.

By its nature, it should be able to protect itself against direct air attack. The larger the carrier, the more defensive aircraft it can carry and operate. Nevertheless, the carrier remains vulnerable to missiles and submarines.

Because large size increases the prospects for such things as the armouring of the flight and lower decks, and the protection of magazines and crew areas, a fleet carrier is much better able to absorb damage than a smaller ship. But large size offers little protection against nuclear attack, and is indeed something of an incentive for it.

For all these reasons, the fleet carrier will need to be well equipped with deception devices and all manner of defensive armament, a factor which, paradoxically, will tend to increase its size, and its cost, still further. It will also need a variety of escorts, and so the emphasis these days is not on the carrier but on the carrier battle group.

(iii)   *Operational Power*. The power of a carrier is largely, though not exclusively, a function of the capacity and number of the aircraft it carries. As far as the US Navy is concerned, the large size of a fleet carrier like the USS *Nimitz* at 81,000 tons standard displacement, eighty to ninety aircraft and a complement of 6300 men, provides an air wing with a four dimensional capacity against air, land, surface and underwater targets. With its load of highly sophisticated aircraft, such as the F-14 *Tomcat* fighter for instance (which is capable of engaging several enemies at once out to a range of a hundred nautical miles) or its A-6 *Intruder* force, the fleet carrier's defensive and offensive power are both truly awesome. They are the ultimate symbol of conventional naval might.

Because it has been so much affected by changing naval technology since 1945, the place of the aircraft carrier in naval warfare, and its particular contribution to the winning of sea control has tended to be the focus of a good deal of debate.

In the immediate postwar period, the US Navy fleet carrier took on the new role of strategic strike. It became a platform from which aircraft armed with nuclear weapons could be launched against the Soviet Union, or indeed against anyone else. For the same reason, countering the US Navy's carriers became an important role for the Soviet Navy.

However, the development of long-range ballistic missile firing submarines took

PLATE 5.9 An EA-3B *Skywarrior* electronic warfare aircraft has just been catapulted from the port side of the *Nimitz*. An F-14A *Tomcat* waits its turn on the starboard catapult.
(US Navy)

PLATE 5.10 The F/A-18 *Hornet* can carry a range of air-to-air and air-to-ground missiles, bombs, ASW weapons, fuel tanks and sensor pods and carries a M-61 six barrel gun in the nose. Such aircraft make large aircraft carriers arguably the most formidable weapon system afloat. (US Navy)

away much of the strategic element of this mission; moreover the advent of nuclear weapons generally seemed to undermine the whole idea of sustained naval warfare for which the fleet carrier seemed so eminently suited. By the mid 1960s, the end of the carrier era appeared to be in sight and the then Secretary of Defense, Robert McNamara, decided that the number of carriers should be allowed to decline, as they approached the end of their operational lives, without compensating replacement.

The Vietnam War caused something of a rethink, as it demonstrated that carriers could still launch quite devastating air strikes against land targets, and might need to. According to Admiral Gorshkov, (whose views on the matter are really quite interesting!) the US Navy launched 200,000 aircraft sorties against Vietnam from April 1965 to December 1968, with one carrier being able to launch 178 strike sorties per day.

Although the carriers' control of the sea was not seriously contested during the Vietnam War, they took all the necessary precautions. They 'manoeuvred in dispersed combat order, were constantly shielded in the air by fighters and took anti-submarine, anti-mine and anti-ship defence measures'. As a result they were able to brush aside the few attacks that developed. In extreme contrast, thousands of aircraft operating from shore bases were damaged or destroyed by ground action; bases to operate them had to be constructed, guarded and ultimately abandoned, complete with all their stores and equipment. The cost-effectiveness of the fleet carrier as an instrument for securing and exerting sea control, and then for projecting power ashore seemed to have been triumphantly demonstrated.

Nevertheless, the sheer cost of these vessels could not be denied. In Britain it led to the decision in 1966 not to proceed with the construction of CVA-01, a new fleet carrier, but instead to opt for a number of much smaller and more austere mini-carriers, which eventually became the *Invincible* class. In the Falklands conflict of 1982, these ships showed themselves to be more than adequate for limited conflicts although, obviously, they were not in the same league as ships like the US Navy's *Nimitz* class. While the British were scaling down, largely for reasons of cost, the Russians were scaling up, because their ambitions for sea control were expanding. After many years of public scepticism about the survivability of large carriers, the Russians produced first the 36,000 ton *Kiev* class of 'heavy aircraft carrying cruiser' and then in 1985 launched what would seem to be the first of a fully fledged fleet carrier class at Nikolayev.

But by far the most interesting debate took place in the United States, where Admiral Elmo Zumwalt took over as Chief of Naval Operations in 1970. Zumwalt decided that the shape of the US Navy had been grossly distorted by the emphasis given to its large, costly, though powerful, carrier fleet and advocated instead, as we have seen, a new 'Hi/Lo' mix where more emphasis would be given instead to cheaper ships of moderate performance, which could be procured in much larger number. The carrier part of this concept was the development of what became

PLATE 5.11 The Soviet *Kiev* class is midway between the *Nimitz* and the *Invincible* class. But at 36,000 tons it is still ten times bigger than the shadowing British *Leander* class frigate *Danae* (MOD (Navy))

known as the 'sea control ship'. In many ways, this was an American version of the British *Invincible* or the Russian *Kiev* classes of small carrier. Sea control ships would not project massive military power against the land or seek to dominate great swathes of the ocean, but would instead be equipped with helicopters and vertical take-off aircraft whose tasks were to guard the maritime force, of which they were a part, against air, surface and submarine activity.

Sea trials eventually cast doubt on the capacity of the sea control ship to protect itself against land based bombers, and the idea was effectively abandoned in the mid 1970s. However, the fleet carrier concept was required to change as well. Some of its strike aircraft were taken away and replaced with squadrons of S-3A *Viking* ASW aircraft and SH-3H *Sea King* ASW helicopters. Both of these moves were intended to help meet the growing menace posed by the modern submarine and to show the extent to which the mission of the carrier is largely a function of the mix of aircraft it carries.

The American controversy about the proper role of the carrier rumbles on however and opinion is by no means unanimous that a few large, expensive but powerful fleet carriers is in fact the best way to go. The particular debate of the Reagan administration, however, has been the extent to which carriers could and should participate in the kind of Forward Operations described above.

On the one hand, sceptics argue that carrier operations around Northern Norway, for instance, would be very hazardous given the extent of possible opposition from Soviet submarines and land-based airpower. A carrier task force, they say, would be hard put to survive, let alone inflict significant damage on Soviet naval or land power. Advocates challenge all this, and argue that their analyses of the likely outcome of the air and submarine battle shows the very reverse. A combined task force of several carrier battle groups would, they conclude, be a very powerful instrument of sea control, even in the most hostile of waters.

This controversy, which is to a large extent the product of differing perceptions of the implications of current and projected technological development for aircraft carriers, will be taken up again later in this series.

The Surface Ship

Many of the same issues re-appear when the present and future prospects of the large surface ship (that is the ship of 2000 tons displacement or more) are considered. Many observers have deduced from such things as the sinking of the Israeli destroyer *Eilat* in 1967 by Egyptian fast attack craft firing their *Styx* missiles from Alexandria harbour, or from the losses suffered by the British Task Force in the Falklands campaign, that surface naval power has significantly eroded over the past several decades.

Their case is that the surface ship is large, visible, slow-moving and expensive in terms of what it can offer, when compared to submarines and aircraft. The offensive power of the surface ship is constrained by the increasing need to devote a large proportion of its displacement tonnnage to the simple business of staying afloat in an increasingly hostile environment. As a result, it has more difficulty in surviving and less capacity to do the enemy harm than it used to have.

As a result it is primarily of use for relatively low-risk tasks like NATO's wartime

PLATE 5.12 The Arab-Israeli wars of 1967 and 1973 and the Indo-Pakistan War of 1971 were among the first to illustrate the impact of the missile on naval operations. Here an Israeli FAC fires a *Gabriel* SSM. Israel was amongst the first Third World countries to build sophisticated naval equipment of its own, and this is plainly a growing tendency. (IDF)

escort of merchant shipping in mid Atlantic where enemy forces would be few, for situations requiring no more than the limited application of force, for flag-showing, training cruises and for holding cocktail parties in foreign ports.

This attack on the present and future validity of the surface ship will be considered under two headings, namely its survivability, and its anticipated role in sea control operations and naval warfare generally.

Surface Ship Survivability. Many experts dispute the view that the surface ship is prohibitively vulnerable. They start by observing that the whole question of whether the surface ship is vulnerable to destruction is fundamentally a relative matter not an absolute one. All weapons systems, be they ships, submarines, aircraft or tanks are vulnerable to destruction in certain sets of circumstances. In this sense, the surface ship of course is vulnerable, but the real question is whether it is so vulnerable that it can no longer perform its tasks.

Survivability is partly a function of the surface ship's capacity to inflict damage, which will be considered under the next heading, and partly to dodge or absorb it. The latter was a particular focus of public debate in the wake of British losses during the Falklands War.

Some commentators concentrated on the effectiveness of Argentine missile and bomb attacks on British ships, arguing that British losses would have been even more severe had Argentine bombs been fused properly. Their conclusion was sometimes that surface ships were floating anachronisms which would have been even more at risk if the Task Force had been confronting opposition of the first rank. Several points can be made to counter this view:

—Ships which were on air picket duty on the open sea, like HMS *Sheffield*, were particularly exposed to long-range missile attack, because of their relatively isolated position, and the low level of air support available to counter hostile aircraft operating from secure land bases. Given these particular disadvantages, the Task Force *did* face 'opposition of the first rank'.

—Ships which were acting in support of amphibious operations, and virtually stationary in land-locked waters were relatively safe from missile attack, but vulnerable to old-fashioned bomb attack. The high ground all around, which protected them from the acquisition radars of incoming *Exocet* missiles, also much reduced warning time of approaching aircraft. Nevertheless, the effectiveness of the British air defence forced the Argentine aircraft to drop their bombs very low. This may have increased bomb-dropping accuracy, but the short interval between

PLATE 5.13 HMS *Sheffield* was the first modern casualty of a naval missile in the Falklands campaign. HMS *Arrow*, a Type 21 frigate comes to her aid. (MOD (Navy)

release and impact was insufficient for the bombs to arm themselves, and this much reduced their effectiveness even when they did hit their targets. The *tactical* effectiveness of British air defence missiles in this conflict was plainly illustrated by much more than the number of aircraft they shot down.

—Despite their losses, the surface warships, did achieve their primary purpose, which was the particularly hazardous one of supporting an amphibious operation within range of hostile air bases. This is another factor which needs to be entered into the survivability equation.

Turning to the question of damage-absorption rather than damage-avoidance, it is certainly true that the modern ship-designer has new and difficult problems to face in this area. One of the most important is that, in broad terms, the centre of gravity of the modern surface ship has moved higher. This is partly because modern propulsion systems, especially gas turbine engines, are much lighter than those of old fashioned steam-powered ships with their heavy boilers. In addition, modern ships have to clutter their superstructures with a great variety of weapons, sensors, aerials and masts. All this iron-mongery, plus the lighter engines, means there is more chance of the ships becoming top-heavy.

To reduce this danger, all sorts of weight reducing measures have been introduced, for instance:

—to reduce, or in the vast majority of cases to do away with altogether, the armour-plating that surface warships used once to carry. The thinness of the hull of modern ships would astonish the ship-designer of the machine age. Like Admiral Fisher's battlecruisers, the modern warship is often 'an eggshell armed with sledgehammers'.

—to use fibre-glass, plastics and alloys of various kinds for as many fittings as possible. For instance accommodation ladders these days are sometimes made not of steel, but of some much lighter, but less strong material.

—to use, wherever possible, aluminium instead of steel since this reduces weight by fifty per cent. Aluminium is used in the superstructure of very many ships around the world, both civil (like the *Queen Elizabeth II*, which has 1400 tons of aluminium in her superstructure) and naval.

The difficulty, of course, is that although they make a considerable contribution to solving the modern warship's stability problems, these materials are often more susceptible to fire and blast, and so reduce the ship's capacity to absorb damage. In the aftermath of the Falklands War, this point was often made in relation to the use of aluminium in Royal Naval warships. The impression w2as sometimes given that these were almost entirely made of aluminium and would melt at the slightest opportunity.

Less exaggeratedly, adverse comparisons were drawn between modern Type 21 frigates (such as HMS *Ardent*) and the older more robust type of warship like HMS *Glamorgan* (which survived an *Exocet* hit with comparatively little structural damage). Instead of building warships that were vulnerable even to modern rifle fire, would it not be better to revert to the defence philosophy exemplified by the *Iowa* class of battleship, recently re-commissioned by the US Navy? These ships can not only inflict damage, but also absorb it. Finally, the point was made that during the Gulf War between Iran and Iraq even oil tankers have proved surprisingly resilient when hit by rockets and missiles. Is there not something odd about a ship design principle which produces warships that are more vulnerable to enemy fire than unarmed merchantmen?

Sceptics about the future of the surface ship argue that ship designers have got themselves into this paradoxical situation because the weapon system they are endeavouring to preserve is fundamentally anachronistic.

Against this, however, measures can, and indeed have, been taken which maintain the stability advantages of the new materials but which reduce associated problems of resilience. The Falklands experience, for example, stimulated much study of ways of improving the surface ship's fire-fighting capabilities, not least by avoiding the use of materials which give off toxic fumes when burning.

The resilience problems of aluminium were known well before the Falklands conflict. Indeed the American cruiser USS *Belknap* collided with another ship in 1975, and had a fire fierce enough to melt her aluminium superstructure. American studies showed that the answer to the problem was first to fit the aluminium with an aluminium silicate cladding which would insulate it against the effects of heat and

PLATE 5.14 Old-fashioned ships like the battleship *New Jersey* have a constructional robustness which would protect them from naval missiles. This was one of the reasons for the reactivation and refitting of the *Iowa* class of battleships by the US Navy. Such battleships will also carry *Tomahawk* cruise missiles with ranges from 250–1500 miles, depending on the variant and the sixty mile *Harpoon* anti-ship missile. (US Navy))

which would give fire-fighters a chance to get the situation under control before the superstructure melted.

The next problem was that, in certain circumstances, the insulation material itself could fragment into dangerous splinters if it was struck by a bomb, missile or shell. To guard against this danger, it was covered with a laminate of 'Kevlar', which is a fire-resistant synthetic fabric.

Naturally, fitting these two materials to the aluminium involved extra cost, more time, and somewhat reduced the weight advantages of using it in the first place. But generally, the advantages are held much to outweigh the disadvantages, and modern US Navy warships, like the new *Aegis* guided missile cruiser and its FFG frigates, continue to make extensive use of protected aluminium in their construction.

This is by no means the only technological problem confronting the surface ship. Others have pointed out that its capacity to do the enemy harm is a function of the offensive power of the weapons it carries. Some sceptics argue that the size and weight of its defensive systems is such that while it may, or may not, survive, its usefulness has markedly declined. A much higher percentage of its effort is now devoted to the simple business of staying afloat. This is a complicated business which will be tackled more extensively later in this series.

PLATE 5.15 The British *Sea Wolf* missile is a close range anti-missile and anti-aircraft missile. The system's surveillance antennae and missile director are visible just behind the launcher. (MOD (Navy))

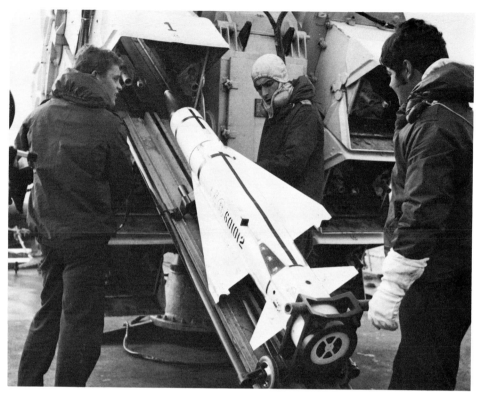

PLATE 5.16 A *Sea Wolf* missile being loaded into its launcher. The system proved effective
in the Falklands campaign, and trials showed it to be capable of hitting incoming 4.5″ shells
at a closing speed in excess of 2.5 Mach. (MOD (Navy))

Survivability: First Conclusions

The general conclusion of ship designers is that the availability of modern
defensive weapons and sensors, like the British air defence missile, *Sea Wolf*, various
electronic deception measures and the latest anti-submarine devices, maintains the
surface ship's capacity to dodge damage. Constructional advances, such as those
discussed above, preserve its capacity to absorb damage, while maintaining its
stability. But few would deny that keeping the surface ship sufficiently survivable in
the nuclear age will remain a problem for the foreseeable future.

It is worth noting, however, that this has always been the case, to a greater or lesser
extent. In the past, as every new technological development or combination of
developments has come along and affected naval operations, there have always been
those who doubted whether the 'traditional' surface warship would survive. So far at
least, the surface warship has survived, though at the price of absorbing radical
changes itself, and becoming a good deal less 'traditional'. At the moment, there is
little sign that this continuous chain of technical challenge and response is about to be
finally broken.

A final, somewhat more nebulous, point should be made here as well. This is to
point out that, in some ways, the survivability of the surface ship is an improper topic
in that naval operations are a team effort by a fleet mixed and balanced in such a way

PLATE 5.17 The US Navy's *Aegis* system is a much more ambitious concept designed to detect, track and engage multiple missile, aircraft, surface and underwater missile threats simultaneously. Here the cruiser USS *Ticonderoga* has just fired a *Standard* missile from its forward launcher. (RCA)

that the different constituent strengths and weaknesses are set against each other. The focus of analysis should be on the working of the team as a whole and not on the individual performance of individual players. Thus, even if the surface ship is more vulnerable than it used to be, and needs to be guarded by other platforms to a greater extent, its retention in the team may still be justified by the contribution it makes to the overall effort. This raises again the issue of what is the role of the modern surface warship.

The Role of the Surface Ship

France's Admiral Moineville has aptly described the surface ship as the foot soldier of the sea. It has the same ubiquity in naval operations as the infantry does on land. It is an essential part of all types of naval activity from contesting sea control to all the various ways of exploiting it that will be addressed later.

Moineville argues that being at once under the surface of the sea, on it and above it, the surface ship can receive all kinds of data, and can make the best possible assessment of any given situation and so participate in all types of action. Certainly, a look at the attack envelopes of a ship like the Soviet Navy's *Kirov* battlecruiser,

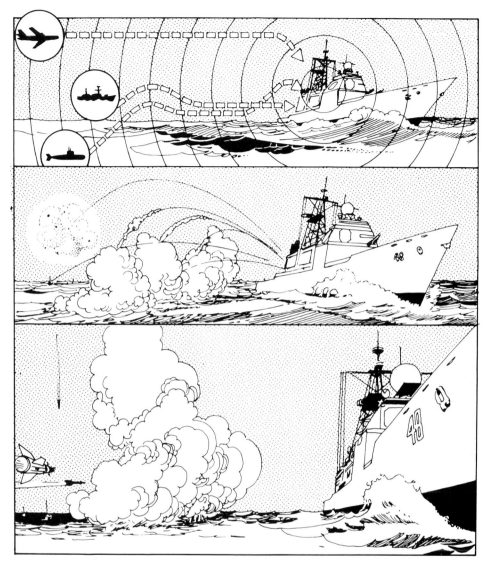

Fɪɢ 5.6 Ship Defences. *Sybil* is a defence system intended to protect ships from all types of missile threat. By dispensing chaff and a variety of decoys, it seduces, distracts and confuses single missiles or groups of missiles fired from submarine, air or surface ship. (Brandt Armaments, France)

demonstrates just how flexible a surface ship with a wide range of onboard weapon systems can be. The surface ship's versatility means that it can act effectively in a whole range of possible actions at sea.

Like other platforms in the battle, it can carry sensors and weaponry appropriate to all four types of activity related to the contest for sea control, namely:

—*Anti-surface warfare*, where it uses its on board or helicopter borne missiles, its guns, torpedoes or mines to attack other surface warships.

—*Anti-submarine warfare*, where surface ships have particular advantages in deploying anti-submarine sensors for long periods of time. The recent advent of effective sonar arrays towed behind surface ships is likely to increase their value for the detection of submarines still further. Ships can also attack submarines directly with a whole variety of anti-submarine weapons launched either from the ship itself, or from its helicopter.

—*Anti-aircraft warfare*, where the ship is not just a potential victim of the air battle but also a factor in the struggle for air superiority. In its capacity to maintain air surveillance, and to shoot aircraft down, the surface ship can make an important contribution to the air defence of naval formations. Until recently, this was the Soviet Navy's only means of defence against air attack when operating outside the range of land-based aircraft.

—*Operations against the shore*. The arrival of long-range naval cruise missiles intended for the attack of land targets is a significant accretion of power for the surface ship. In some cases the land targets in question, for example air and naval bases, radar stations and the like may be directly relevant to the struggle for sea control.

Admiral Moineville concludes,

Thus missiles, data processing and helicopters have restored standard surface ships to their rightful place in combat at sea—something that would have seemed unlikely some years ago.

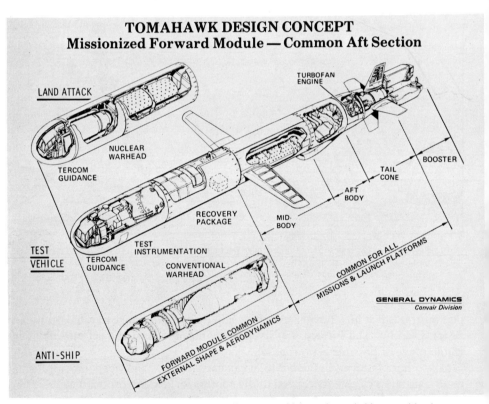

TOMAHAWK DESIGN CONCEPT
Missionized Forward Module — Common Aft Section

PLATE 5.18 The SSM *Tomahawk* is a versatile system which can be anti-ship or anti-land, with a nuclear or conventional warhead. It represents a considerable increase in the capacity of the surface ship to attack land targets. (General Dynamics)

In short, by its capacity to act in these four spheres of sea control related operations, the surface ship offers another layer on the offensive and defensive capacities of the fleet. Moreover, it has unique advantages to offer in the area of command and control, and has greater sustainability and 'loiter time' than most aircraft.

A final more philosophical point needs to be made as well. Maritime warfare is essentially a struggle for control of the sea so that its resources may be exploited, and use made of it for the transport of people and materials or the projection of power ashore. These are all positive sea uses; few nations can afford to restrict themselves merely to negative 'sea denial' operations. Unless the day comes when supplies can all be carried by submarine, or military assaults exclusively by air, surface ships are plainly necessary for positive sea use. So much is this the case, that the claim that surface ships have had their day, effectively means that sea control, and sea power has had it too.

THE NATURE OF BATTLE

This survey of the effect that evolving naval technology has had on the all-important function of sea control will conclude with a brief look at the nature of modern battle. For a basic authority, we will take the writings of Admiral Gorshkov.

'The battle,' he says, 'always was and remains the main means of solving tactical tasks.'

But while its fundamental purpose may remain the same, its character will most definitely change as new technological developments appear. Even so, combat at sea

PLATE 5.19 One of the Royal Navy's versatile new 3500 ton Type 22 frigates, HMS *Broadsword* carries *Exocet* SSM, *Sea Wolf* SAM, two 40 mm guns, homing ASW torpedoes and two *Lynx* helicopters. The visibility of the struts of the hull testifies to the modern warship's lack of armour. (MOD (Navy))

will tend to take certain forms, that are recognisable from era to era. Very often there are three phases to a battle:

First, a period when the main task is to find the enemy.

Second, a period of manoeuvre when forces are deployed tactically.

Third, a series of strikes after the weapons platforms have been brought to bear.

   While new technology may not have done much to change this, it has had a number of important effects—or so Gorshkov believes.

> —*Importance of the first salvo*. The fragility of modern ships, and most particularly of their sensors, means that the advantage of hitting first will grow. The battle for the first salvo will be increasingly decisive for the outcome of the battle as a whole, because the victim has less prospects of recovery, especially if nuclear weapons are used. This fits in very well with the traditional Soviet stress on the often overwhelming advantages of surprise in all forms of military action.
>
> The Soviet Navy has tried out these ideas for real in some of the confrontations it has had with the US 6th Fleet in the Mediterranean. High value units of the US Navy, like aircraft carriers, have been closely accompanied by Soviet 'tattletales' which are expected to relay the unit's position to the rest of the fleet, and very often, are expected to try to get the first shot in, if ever this should be necessary.
>
> Their vulnerability to this kind of surprise attack has led many naval officers around the world to press for more permissive rules of engagement (at least in times of tension) which approach notions of 'anticipatory self-defence'. The notion of hitting an adversary because you believe he is about to hit you is encouraged by certain characteristics of modern technology and could make it more difficult to control naval forces in a crisis.
>
> On the other hand, technological advances, leading to significant improvements in the capacity of naval forces to defend themselves against attack, such as those exemplified by the air defence capacities of the US Navy's *Aegis* cruisers, could be very important in countering this trend.
>
> —*Increased range*. The increasing range of modern maritime weapons systems means that naval battles will be conducted between sets of naval forces at ever increasing distance from one another. This development was of course readily apparent during the machine age, and culminated in the Battle of the Coral Sea in 1942, when Japanese and American aircraft carriers engaged each other in what Admiral Gorshkov calls a 'non-contact battle'. This increases the objective problem of locating the enemy and of maintaining control over the subsequent flow of events.
>
> —*Multi-dimensional battle*. Modern developments have accelerated the historical trend in which battle at sea involves increasingly diverse sets of forces, involving different units on the surface, then underwater, and then in the air. Admiral Gorshkov's successor as Commander-in-Chief of the Soviet Navy, Admiral Chernarvin, has put it like this:
>
>> Under modern conditions, a naval battle represents a combination of strikes by heterogeneous forces . . . (with) . . . regard to target, place and time, and the precision of the cooperation of these forces acquires ever greater and greater significance in battle.
>
> Soviet naval exercises show that a simulated enemy will be attacked by diverse

forces, namely submarines firing missiles or torpedoes, aircraft of various types and surface ships, either in sequence, or in conjunction. In both cases, the objective will be to overwhelm the enemy's defences by the sheer number of weapons launched and by the variety of their flight path.

The idea behind this is not of course new, for, after all, aviators have always recognised the advantages of attacking naval targets in two different ways (say, by torpedo-dropping and dive-bombing aircraft) at the same time since this would confuse the target's fighter and gunfire defence and so enhance prospects of success. But modern developments mean that the extent to which this is possible has grown considerably.

In the Soviet view, it confirms the necessity for a properly balanced fleet offering as many attack (and come to that, defence) options as possible. This emphasis on the orchestration of diverse forces of air, surface and sub-surface units, over possibly extensive stretches of water, implies a particular need for a sophisticated and resilient system of command-and-control.

A general problem faced by the larger navies in this respect is that measures designed to cope with one type of naval warfare might be quite inappropriate for another. For instance, close tactical positioning is a good idea when coping with the prospects of conventional air attack since this increases prospects for mutual support. It is, however, the last thing a naval commander will want to do if confronted with the possibility of nuclear or some other form of area attack. It will be the task of the resourceful commander to exploit his opponent's uncertainties to the maximum in this regard.

Scope. The intensity of the battle will increase because of the growth in the relative effectiveness of various means of attack; this factor is particularly apparent in the case of nuclear weapons at sea, but is generally true as well. Because of this, Admiral Gorshkov argues, speed, manoevrability and dispersion of forces will be more and more necessary. Instead of a battle fleet proceeding in stately line ahead, as was once the case in days of sail, the modern fleet will be spread over a huge area of the ocean, and much of it extremely active for short sharp periods of time.

This reinforces the need for an effective command-and-control system, lest the cohesiveness of the force be lost. The command-and-control system itself becomes an important element of the fleet, something which could be attacked by a resourceful enemy, and something which could be a source of tactical and strategic vulnerability if the balance between centralised control and local initiative were upset. For this reason, the Russians believe that electronic support measures to interfere with an adversary's command-and-control system, and to protect one's own, are a very important characteristic of the fleet indeed.

In this regard, reconnaissance and intelligence gathering satellites are regarded as an important constituent of the fleet. Their activity and measures to protect or destroy them will therefore be an important element in the battle for sea control.

The vulnerability of the electronic sinews of modern command-and-control systems to the electro-magnetic pulse associated with nuclear explosions is another important factor to be taken into account. Such disruption would make sustained naval activity of any sort in a nuclear environment more difficult; in particular it would complicate the control and limitation of subsequent nuclear operations. Both of these possible consequences would seem to be important disincentives to the use of such weapons. However, the same possibilities also encourage efforts to 'harden' command-and-control procedures.

CONCLUSIONS

This survey of the impact of technology on the conduct of the Sea Control mission has been quite extensive, because the mission itself is at the epicentre of most naval activity. Upon its success in this vital area will depend a navy's capacity to use the sea to further the strategic interests of the state it serves and to prevent an adversary from doing likewise. The perceived capacity to do this will, in peacetime, have important consequences too.

Since sea control is a relative, rather than absolute, thing, its problems and prospects apply not just to the superpowers but to all countries with any pretension to use the sea for their advantage in peace and in war. Accordingly the technological preoccupations noted in this chapter tend to be those of all navies, to a greater or lesser extent.

6

Navies and Strategic Deterrence

In the last chapter, we explored the concept of sea control and found that it means the capacity to use the sea for one's own purposes and to prevent the enemy from doing the same. It is generally agreed that for a handful of modern navies, their single most important maritime task is the operation of their strategic nuclear deterrent forces.

NUCLEAR DETERRENCE: THE AIM OF THE EXERCISE

Although the precise justification for nuclear deterrent forces may vary from country to country, the general object would seem to be broadly the same, at least for Western states. In broad-brush terms, this is to deter an adversary from launching a full-scale attack by threatening what he will find unacceptable damage in retaliation. Put simply, there are two variants of nuclear deterrence:

1. *Minimum Deterrence*. The most obvious attack to be deterred is a large scale nuclear one directed against the homelands. Here the justification for one side to have nuclear weapons comes close to being merely to deter the other side from using theirs, although this is often not explicitly spelled out, lest it encourage the adversary to launch some kind of less absolute attack

2. *Extended Deterrence*. Alternatively, the nuclear deterrent may be expected to cover other contingencies as well. It may be extended to cover not just the national homeland but also the territory of close allies. It may equally be extended to other forms of direct attack; it may even be regarded as a method of reversing a losing situation in some tactical or theatre battlefield. Plainly, both the Superpowers ascribe to this form of deterrence.

Most analysts argue that nuclear deterrence is just one end of a general spectrum of deterrence. They argue, in many cases rather strongly, that the nuclear variety shades into the less apocalyptic parts of the spectrum in a gradual and imperceptible way. The resultant 'seamless web' of deterrence therefore covers all measures designed to prevent an adversary from doing something by the promise of unacceptable retribution if he does. This spectrum of general deterrence is therefore expected to cover all eventualities, from a full-scale assault at one end of the scale, to, at the other, the most minor infringements of one state's interests by another. It works by the promise of retaliation on a rising scale, ending in the delivery of a nuclear counter-attack.

DETERRENCE AT SEA

Navies are involved in the business of deterrence in two ways. First, they have important roles to play in the general spectrum of deterrence. This is because threats to the interests of the state they serve may well develop at sea. Indeed, given the rising economic and strategic dependence of many countries upon the sea, the incidence of such maritime threats shows little sign of significant decline. Alternatively, it may well be that a capacity to respond at sea is seen as an appropriate way to deal with a variety of non-maritime threats.

General Deterrence

General maritime deterrence of this sort is not, of course, an identifiable task that ships are specifically designed for. Nor can fleets go out and practice it in the way they might conduct, for example, anti-submarine exercises. Instead it comes simply as a preventative variant of the many war-time tasks and functions they *are* designed to carry out. Potential adversaries are deterred, or not deterred, by demonstrations of a navy's evident ability to perform conventional maritime 'war-fighting' tasks efficiently. This is something to be borne in mind when we come on to consider these war-fighting tasks later.

Nuclear Deterrence at Sea

The second way in which navies are involved in the business of deterrence comes from the fact that they are important agencies for the conduct of deterrence at the nuclear end of the scale. They provide important means by which nuclear strikes may be launched at the territory of an adversary.

In the early 1950s, the main naval contribution to the nuclear deterrent task was by means of US Navy strike carriers operating nuclear-capable aircraft within range of the territory of possible adversaries. The Soviet Navy certainly took this threat sufficiently seriously to devote a large proportion of its naval effort to countering it. Later on, the ballistic missile firing submarine took over as the main naval weapon system dedicated to the task. Generally speaking, these weapons are regarded as 'strategic' in the sense that they would have an immediate and decisive influence on any war they are unable to prevent.

But at the same time there have also been a variety of 'tactical' or 'theatre' nuclear weapons at sea. The expectation is that the use of smaller nuclear weapons like these would have immediate impact, respectively, on the outcome of a specific battle or campaign. Into this category would come nuclear depth bombs for use against submarines, nuclear-tipped torpedoes or anti-ship missiles and land-attack cruise missiles with nuclear warheads.

Of course the difference between the three categories of maritime nuclear weapons is far from sharp, not least because the label we attach to them is at least as much a function of how they are used as it is of their intrinsic characteristics; moreover, there may be considerable differences in perception of such matters between the attacker and the victim. For the United States, a nuclear cruise missile attack on the Soviet Baltic Fleet's Zhdanov shipyard might be regarded as a 'theatre' strike; but as far as the residents of Leningrad were concerned it would seem decidedly strategic. More to the point, the Soviet government might well choose to interpret the attack in that light, and respond accordingly. Moreover in some circumstances an apparently 'strategic' system like a ballistic missile firing submarine *could* be used as a theatre or possibly even a tactical system if it launched its missiles against a naval air base, or naval formation at sea.

Putting the Deterrent to Sea

For the time being, however, we will concentrate on the maritime instruments of *strategic* deterrence. There are many advantages in putting the strategic deterrent at sea in nuclear propelled ballistic missile firing submarines (SSBNs). Admiral Gorshkov lists four:

1. It increases reach, because SSBNs can use the sea to approach their target more closely. This was a particular advantage in the 1950s and the 1960s when the range of missiles was limited.
2. It means that attacks can be made from different directions, which complicates the adversary's task in trying to counter them. Even now, when the increased range of sea-launched missiles makes it no longer necessary, there are advantages in approaching an adversary's shore-line quite closely and launching missiles on a depressed trajectory since this greatly reduces flight time and warning. This may be of advantage against time-sensitive targets like bomber bases, for example.
3. Putting a large proportion of the nuclear deterrent force at sea reduces the adversary's incentive to launch disarming strikes against the homeland. Since the collateral damage, to cities and population, of such disarming strikes could easily be enormous, this is an important advantage.
4. Most significantly, however, putting nuclear missiles in SSBNs is the best currently available method of concealing them. This means the SSBN offers what, at the moment, would seem to be the best prospect of a nuclear deterrent force which will be largely secure against enemy action and therefore always available as a final means of retaliation. Whatever an aggressor does, and however skilfully he plans his attack, he will not therefore be able to escape retribution. Since the whole philosophy of deterrence through 'mutual assured destruction' (MAD) rests on this principle, the Navy, says Gorshkov, has become 'a most important factor deterring his nuclear attack.'

SSBN Methods of Operation

Technological change has brought important changes to the way that navies have conducted the strategic deterrent mission, and will no doubt continue to do so. So far, the most important change has come about as a result of the development of ballistic missile firing submarines, whose *modus operandi* is quite different from the nuclear armed strikes carriers that preceded them.

In approximate terms, this table represents the SSBNs currently engaged in this role.

TABLE 6.1 *Ballistic Missile Firing Submarines*

Soviet Union

Sub Type	No.	No. of Missiles	Total Missiles
Typhoon	4	20 × SS-N-20	80
Delta IV	2	16 × SS-N-23	32
Delta III	14	16 × SS-N-18	224
Delta II	4	16 × SS-N-8	64
Delta I	18	12 × SS-N-8	216
Yankee II	1	12 × SS-N-17	12
Yankee I	19	16 × SS-N-6	304
	62[1]		932[1]

United States

Sub Type	No.	No. of Missiles	Total Missiles
Ohio	8	24 × Trident C4	192
Lafayette	16 }	{ 16 × Poseidon C3	256
Franklin	12 }	16 × Trident C4	192
	37		640

France

Sub Type	No.	No. of Missiles	Total Missiles
L'Inflexible	1	16 × M4	16
Le Redoutable	1	16 × M4	16
	4	16 × M2	64
	6		96

Britain

Sub Type	No.	No. of Missiles	Total Missiles
Resolution	4	16 × Polaris A3	64
	4		64

China

Sub Type	No.	No. of Missiles	Total Missiles
Xia	2	12 × JL-1	24
	2[2]		24[2]

Notes:
[1] Soviet figures exclude old Golf and Hotel class SSB(N)s.
[2] Chinese figures are very uncertain.
(Source: *International Institute for Strategic Studies, The Military Balance 1986–1987.*)

At the moment, there are three main methods of deploying SSBNs in the strategic deterrent role:

1. Individual Forward Deployment

In this mode of operation, SSBNs make maximum use of the concealment possibilities of the ocean itself. They operate essentially as lone wolves, avoiding contact with all other naval forces to the greatest extent possible. Stealth is their main defence.

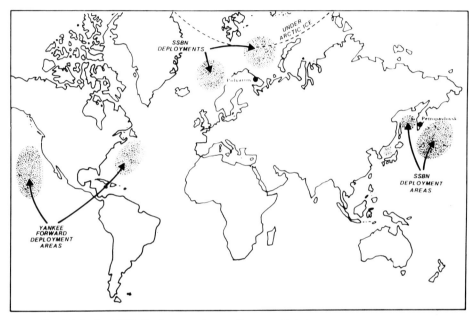

Fig 6.1 Soviet SSBN Deployment Areas. (Source: US DOD, *Soviet Military Power*)

In broad terms this mode of operation is typical of Western SSBN forces and, in the early 1960s, when the range of the missiles they carried was limited to 1300 miles or so, *Polaris* submarines had to approach the coast of their adversary quite closely, and would not expect direct support from the rest of the fleet.

As the range of submarine launched ballistic missiles (SLBMs) has gradually extended to 4500 miles and more, the physical need to approach the enemy's coast has obviously declined. As we have just seen, however, there remain possible *operational* reasons why SSBNs may seek to come closer to hostile shores than the range of their missiles may make strictly necessary.

When the SSBN operates on its own, either forward-deployed or not, the only direct support it would expect of the rest of the fleet would be 'sanitisation' operations in the approaches to its base. Here the idea would be to clear the area of enemy submarines, so that they could not latch on to a SSBN as it comes out and trail as it sets off on patrol. It would be equally necessary to make sure that the base

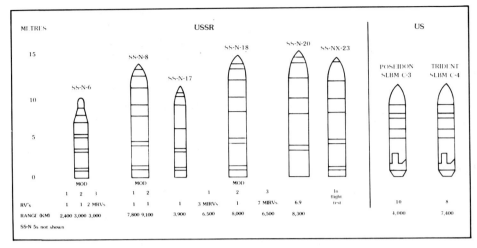

FIG 6.2 Submarine Launched Ballistic Missiles (SLBMs) (Source: US DOD, *Soviet Military Power*)

approaches, or obvious SSBN transit lines, were not mined or sown with detection devices.

Of course, in a more general way, the SSBN, even when operating on its own, would expect a good deal of *indirect* support from the fleet. Every hostile ASW aircraft, surface ship and submarine destroyed by the fleet in the course of its own operations is one less possible source of threat to the lone SSBN.

A good deal of this applies to the Soviet Navy too. Soviet *Yankee* submarines suffered from the limited range of their SLBMs in that, in order to be able to attack the territory of the United States, they had to launch their missiles from relatively exposed positions in the Western Atlantic and Eastern Pacific. Moreover, to get there, they had to pass through geographic narrows (most obviously the Greenland-

PLATE 6.1 Three of the French Navy's five SSBNs of the *Le Redoutable* class. With a surface displacement of 8000 tons, these submarines carry sixteen M20 missiles each. The range of the M20 missile is about 1500 nautical miles, but it is being replaced by the 4000 mile M 4 missile. (French Navy)

Iceland-United Kingdom (GIUK) gap) where they could expect to encounter opposition from Western ASW forces.

For this reason, Admiral Gorshkov, in his various writings has put considerable stress on the need for the rest of the fleet, submarines, aircraft and surface ships too, to help the Soviet SSBNs get out onto the open sea. This operational disadvantage, which is largely a product of geography, explains why the Soviet Navy has devoted so much effort to the production of far longer range SLBMs. With missiles like the 8300 km SS-N-20, Soviet SSBNs do not need to deploy forwards and so may avoid many of these relative disadvantages.

Nevertheless forward and individual deployments continue by Soviet SSBNs. Four reasons have been suggested for this:

—It may simply be because there are still a number of *Yankee* submarines in the Soviet Navy's inventory.

—It may be for such special operational reasons as was discussed earlier in connection with diversified or depressed trajectory launches.

—It may be essentially political in that forward deployed missile firing submarines are represented by the Soviet authorities as an 'analogous response' to the deployment of Cruise Missiles and *Pershing IIs* in Western Europe. In short they are a 'theatre' weapon and not a strategic one.

—Finally, it has been argued that forward deployment is a response to water space management problems nearer home. As Admiral Harry S. Train, then

PLATE 6.2 The 9300 ton Soviet *Yankee* class of SSBN began to arrive in the fleet in 1967. It carries sixteen 1600 mile SS-N-6 missiles in two rows of eight. (MOD (Navy))

Supreme Allied Commander Atlantic remarked in 1982, 'As they use up the sea space available to them in the northern Norwegian Sea and the Barents Sea, it is quite likely that they will start to station some of their *Delta* submarines in the South Atlantic, perhaps in the Narrows between Brazil and Africa.' The point here is that, to avoid accidental attacks and so forth, SSBNs are given designated patrol areas, and the Soviet Navy may simply be running out of room!

2. Fleet Deployment

This idea is particularly characteristic of the Soviet Navy. Instead of relying primarily on its own stealthiness, or on the size and concealment possibilities of the oceans, the SSBN seeks security through the direct support of the rest of the fleet.

Most analysts argue that the Soviet Navy has developed 'bastion areas' mainly in the Sea of Okhotsk and the Barents Sea. These bastions are very close to the Soviet Union which makes it easier for the Soviet Navy to turn them into areas that are very hostile indeed for Western ASW forces. In particular, proximity facilitates:

—Detailed mapping of the underwater configuration of the area, so the navy has all the advantage that an army gets through fighting on home ground.
—Extensive use of the sea bed for detection systems and defensive mining.
—Heavy patrolling of the area by submarines, surface ships and aircraft.
—Shore support for all forces engaged in this pro-SSBN mission.

Although, no doubt, Soviet SSBNs will seek to hide from any Western ASW forces that do nevertheless manage to penetrate these heavily defended areas, the principle of this mode of operation is different from individual deployments in one essential respect. In this case, certain disadvantages in being easier to locate are accepted, because they are outweighed by the advantages of much better direct protection. In effect, Western ASW forces may have a better chance of finding Soviet SSBNs (because they are concentrated in a relatively restricted sea area) but much less chance of doing very much about it (because they are so heavily defended).

3. Under-ice Deployment

This third method of SSBN deployment is the newest. It involves making the maximum use of the concealment possibilities of the ice, especially of the Arctic. The noises made by ice flows grinding together around the rim of the ice-cap, and the dense and complicated profiles of large masses of ice make most technical means of submarine detection much more difficult. A modern SSBN, perhaps like the Soviet *Typhoon* class could possibly wedge itself into some concealed position in a large ice-mass, possibly just drifting around with it, could break loose and fire its missiles either through inner ice or through the many water gaps there are even in the main ice-cap, when it needed to.

The operational consequences of this method of SSBN deployment could be very significant, especially in two regards,

—detection would be intrinsically more difficult and an adversary inclined to

PLATE 6.3 An artist's impression of a Soviet *Typhoon* submarine launching one of its long-range SS-N-20 missiles, underwater and underway. (US DOD)

engage in anti-SSBN operations would need ASW technology of the most ambitious type to counter the unique problems of dealing with ice.

—for the same reason, the SSBN's need for direct support from the rest of the fleet, while not disappearing altogether, would be much reduced. This means that this method of SSBN deployment would release a large proportion of the rest of the Soviet Navy to go elsewhere and do other things.

ANTI-SSBN OPERATIONS

Because the task of maintaining the sea-based part of the strategic nuclear deterrent tends to have top priority in the countries that have this capability, the forces that conduct it are usually amongst the first to receive and be affected by emerging technology. Exactly the same thing applies to those forces which are expected to offer a defence against SSBNs.

But before we look at the way that new technology has affected and continues to affect anti-SSBN operations, we should consider the possible implications of a decision to devote the new technology to this task in the first place.

The Consequences of Success?

What would happen if SSBNs turned out to be vulnerable to the new technology and the tactics it inspired? Amongst the possible consequences often pointed out are:

—It might undermine the credibility of national deterrent systems like those of France, China or Britain, which rest on small numbers of SSBNs. This, in turn,

might lead them to abandon their SSBNs, adapt them, or increase their number.
—It might increase incentives to conduct nuclear counterforce operations at sea (by attacking SSBNs), because this would cause far less collateral damage in dead and wounded people and irradiated real estate than similar attempts against land-based missiles.
—It might so worry the country whose SSBNs are so threatened that it would devote extra forces to their protection. These forces would not therefore be available for other maritime operations. In some cases, this essentially indirect benefit of anti-SSBN operations might be the main reason for conducting them.
—More worryingly, it might undermine the basic principle of mutual assured destruction (MAD) on which the structure of nuclear deterrence is widely assured to have rested for the past few decades. The argument goes like this.

MAD relies upon both sides feeling that however cleverly they might plan their attack on the enemy's homeland, they would have to face devastating retaliation from his surviving nuclear forces. In theory, this knowledge should prevent any such attack.

As we have seen, the SSBN, has, until now at any rate, been generally regarded as the least likely type of nuclear deterrent forces to be destroyed by a surprise attack. As a result it offers one of the best guarantees of the certainty of the aggressor having to face the prospect of unbearable retaliation. In effect, the SSBN can be regarded as a kind of invulnerable strategic reserve, a secure rataliatory weapon of last resort and thus one form of stability in an otherwise dangerously volatile world. So anything that threatens SSBNs also threatens current philosophies of nuclear deterrence. (There are strategists who argue that nuclear deterrence could and indeed should rest on principles other than MAD, but this is another story!)

—The simultaneous destruction of all hostile SSBNs would be necessary for a totally effective disarming strike, and in theory at any rate, it should be synchronised with an equivalent effort against land-based systems too. In practice, this would seem to be beyond any country's technological reach at the present time. Much more likely would be a partially successful anti-SSBN campaign involving the destruction over a period of time of just a proportion of the enemy's SSBN force. This, it is often said, would give a country facing such an attack every incentive to use its SSBNs before it lost them. An anti-SSBN campaign might therefore precipitate a nuclear holocaust.
—Alternatively, an anti-SSBN campaign which threatened either to degrade an adversary's SSBN force, or which actually did so in war, could act as an effective deterrent because it would threaten an important and valued element in the adversary's deterrent system.

On the face of it, some of these possible consequences of the use of new technology against SSBNs seems good and some bad, either for the defender, the attacker or indeed for both. Which would predominate in a given situation would be a matter of fine judgement. Some analysts believe that the likely bad consequences would certainly outweigh the good in almost all circumstances, and so suggest that the maritime powers agree between themselves not to do it, not to prepare for it but instead to make it a priority area for maritime arms control.

Other analysts are more relaxed about the possible consequences of an anti-SSBN campaign, and suggest that an evident capacity to wage one would offer an effective deterrent in peace and a sensible strategy in war. Whether a country decides to launch a deliberate campaign against hostile SSBNs depends in large measure on which results it thinks most desirable and most likely to occur. Given the current and projected state of the relevant technology, these judgements are likely to remain difficult ones for the forseeable future.

Another point that needs to be made here is that SSBNs may occasionally be prosecuted inadvertently, perhaps in the course of a general anti-submarine campaign fought in some other context. The likelihood of such accidental encounters is of course a function of the relative inexactitude of ASW technology and tactics, and it is to this that we should finally turn.

TECHNOLOGY AND THE ASW BATTLE

It is worth noting that while in this chapter we will be dealing with the technology and tactics of ASW in the context primarily of the hunting of ballistic missile firing submarines, most of it applies just as much to operations against all other types of submarines as well. For the most part, ASW directed against SSBNs is not *sui generis*.

The success of all kinds of anti-submarine operations is a function of a number of variables. Amongst them are:

1. *The State of the Sea*. The physical characteristics of the sea help conceal submerged objects. The opaqueness of masses of water means that detection is largely done by sound, and not sight. Accordingly acoustics has, so far at least, dominated ASW and seems likely to continue to do so. Water is a good conductor of sound and low frequency sounds may be heard thousands of miles from their source. The propagation of sound may be affected by the depth, salinity, temperature and internal movement of water, and by any combination of these and other factors.

The extent to which submarine sounds can be heard also depends on the amount of background noise and on the relative ability of the sensor to filter it out. This is often difficult because with the clattering of stones dragged across a rocky sea-bed, with the myriad sounds of marine life, with ice-floes grinding together and with all the uproar of man's varied uses of the sea, the ocean is a very noisy place and an efficient submarine commander may deliberately choose to hide near such sounds.

The physical shape of the sea bed may be very relevant too. The seventy-five per cent of the world's surface which is covered by water rather than air is, in many ways, analogous to the remainder which is not. It too has mountain ranges, rocky plateaux, deep valleys and crevasses. Parts of it are covered by a primeval sludge, others by moving deserts of sand, still others by forests of kelp and coral. In the currents, storms and shifting temperatures, the water is subject to much the same kind of 'weather' as is the air. Because all these geophysical factors have a considerable bearing on the conduct of ASW operations, knowing the ground is at least as important in sea warfare as it is on land. The extent of its huge hydrographic fleet, suggests that the Soviet Navy, for one, is perfectly well aware of this fact.

2. *The Operational Scenario* will also have a large bearing on the nature of the ASW battle. In this chapter, we are mainly considering the pursuit of the SSBN; but

PLATE 6.4 A 6000 ton Soviet *Victor III* submarine. Nuclear-propelled, this modern submarine began to appear in 1978 and is believed to carry six tubes for torpedoes and anti-submarine missiles. They may soon be equipped with land attack cruise missiles.
(MOD (Navy))

ASW in fact is more likely to be conducted against other types of submarines, specifically against nuclear propelled submarines (SSNs) which either fire missiles, like the Soviet *Charlie* and *Oscar* classes or torpedoes, like the *Victor* class; alternatively, the ASW operation could be against diesel powered submarines like the *Foxtrot* and *Tango* classes, whose main weapon is the torpedo. As we have already seen, nuclear propelled submarines have tended so far to be larger and noisier than diesel ones, although the differences between the two types are likely to diminish in the future.

The range of the missiles carried dictates how closely the submarine carrying them need to approach their targets, which are generally surface ships. Taking the Soviet Navy, once more as an example of the development of submarine technology, early Soviet naval missiles needed the assistance of another platform for final direction to the target, and the vulnerability of these third party platforms weakened the operational effectiveness of the system as a whole. But we must expect improvements in the range of such missiles (which in the case of those carried by the *Oscar* class is already in excess of 250 miles) and a reduction in their need for external assistance.

Torpedo-firing submarines generally need to approach their targets, which may be surface vessels, or indeed other submarines, much more closely. Their offensive effectiveness is partly a function of how many torpedoes they carry.

In the light of all this, the parameters of the battle would obviously be much affected by the nature of the submarine being hunted.

The arena in which the battle is fought would also be important. ASW operations may be offensive operations conducted well forward, defensive ones fought in rear areas or in the presence of military or merchant shipping; they may be over large stretches of open ocean, or in coastal waters; they may be conducted in shallow water or in deep. All these operational variables could be important parts of the overall equation.

3. *Available ASW Technology.* The two essential characteristics of ASW operations, however are the search phase and the attack phase. Search is normally carried out by means of active or passive sonar. The first involves transmitting pulses

into the water and listening for the echo as they bounce off a submarine. It has the merit of being unaffected by the quietness of the target submarine, but the disadvantage of revealing the hunter who propagates the noise as much as the

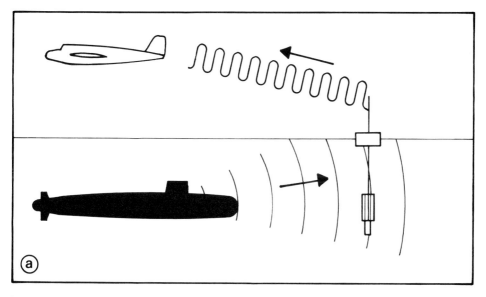

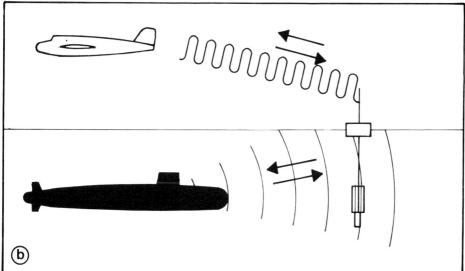

FIG 6.3 Sonar Detection of Submarines. (a) shows a sonobuoy detecting a submarine by picking up the noise generated by the submarine itself. The acoustic detector is suspended below the buoy, often at great depths: data is then relayed to an aircraft above. As submarines become quieter, passive methods of this sort will get more difficult. (b) shows the aircraft ordering the sonobuoy actively to transmit an acoustic signal which is reflected back from the submarine. The consequent information is then relayed to the aircraft. The problem with active methods of detection is that they tell the submarine it is being looked for, and approximately where the transmitter is. In many cases active sonar search could therefore be tactically hazardous.

hunted. Also a great deal of skill is required to diagnose the nature of the echo, so as to distinguish those reflected by hostile submarines from the echoes caused by other things, like passing whales.

Passive sonars simply listen for the noises of passing submarines, propellors, engines, pumps and so on. Search may be carried out over large areas by means of fixed passive sonar arrays connected to shore by cables like the American SOSUS Sound Surveillance System or the Soviet equivalent. The function of these systems is to indicate the rough area of a hostile submarine to various mobile platforms so that they can locate it more accurately. Being fixed, they are vulnerable to enemy attack.

This has encouraged Western navies to investigate alternative area search systems. Currently, one of the most promising of such systems is the towed array that may be deployed and pulled along by surface warships and submarines. The length of the array, and its distance from the noise of the towing platform, make it possible to detect submarines accurately many tens of miles away.

In the United States there is interest in other systems like SURTASS (Surface Ship Towed Array Surveillance System) which are long cables pulled around the sea by civilian manned ships and RDSS (Rapidly Deployable Surveillance System) a method which envisages the fast laying of fields of semi-permanent sonobuoys. The Soviet Union has competing systems with a comparable function but are generally thought to be of inferior performance. The West appears to retain a lead in area search technology, but with the quietening of Soviet submarines, passive sonar will certainly get more difficult.

These area search systems are intended to provide general indicators of a submarine's position to other mobile platforms which will then identify its position

PLATE 6.5 Land-based maritime patrol aircraft are extensively used to locate and prosecute submarines. The *P-3 Orion* is one of the most widely used, and is in service all over the world. It has been flying for over twenty years, but with the aid of constant technical up-dating is still regarded as one of the best such aircraft. The great advantage of MPA is their range and endurance. The range of the *Orion* is some 2500 km, plus four hours on station. (US Navy)

more closely. But it may well be that, in certain circumstances, these mobile platforms will do the whole job themselves. This could apply to maritime patrol aircraft or submarines or surface warships charged with the undersea surveillance of particular sea areas, like enemy bases, chokepoints, geographic narrows and so on. It could also apply to all these ASW units if they were, for example, responsible for the protection of a specific group of military or civilian shipping from hostile submarines.

Surface ships, submarines and land- or ship-based aircraft conducting localised ASW search operations have a variety of active and passive sonars which may be hull-mounted, lowered into the sea, or indeed towed behind the platform. There is a considerable need to orchestrate all these diverse activities into a single integrated data system and the West's technological lead in information technology in the computer and satellite fields, for instance, is an important advantage for ASW operations.

PLATE 6.6 The *Sea King* Mk 5 of the Royal Navy is an ASW helicopter equipped with sonar, sonobuoy dispensing equipment, radar and magnetic detection equipment to help its crew first locate submarines and then attack them with torpedoes or depth charges. (MOD (Navy))

OTHER MEANS OF ATTACK

The last stage of the ASW process is the final attack of the submarine by means of depth charges or depth bombs and various sorts of torpedo and anti-submarine missile launched from aircraft, submarines and surface ships:

Depth Bombs/Charges

There are many depth bombs and depth charges of various sorts which function more or less as they used to in the Second World War. But some may carry nuclear warheads. If the use of nuclear weapons were authorised, they would most likely be used when the submarine was so deep that other ASW weaponry could not reach it physically, or its exact position was unknown. The very deep-diving Soviet *Alpha* submarine is widely believed to pose such a challenge. Leaving aside the attendant dangers of escalation, the use of nuclear weapons at sea could well have serious operational costs as well as benefits. The shock effect would be very widespread and consequent changes to the sea-bed and the structure of the water could prove very difficult to deal with afterwards—at least for a time.

Mortars

Alternatively, a submarine may choose to rest on the bottom, a device which makes detection by torpedoes with active sonar almost impossible. In such cases the use of traditional mortar type weapons would be appropriate, as recent operations in the territorial waters of Sweden and Norway have demonstrated.

Torpedoes

Torpedoes fired by and against submarines are very effective weapons these days. Modern ones are fitted with their own micro-processors, sonar, wake discriminators and have improved explosive charges. They can be fired at ranges in excess of fifteen nautical miles. Western systems like the Australian *Ikara*, the American *Asroc* and the French *Malafon* (and the equivalent Soviet system the SS-N-14) are surface launched guided missiles which carry a homing torpedo.

Base Attack

Additionally, submarines, SSBNs included, are to an extent vulnerable to attack in their home bases or in the approaches to them. The fact that the Soviet Navy deploys on average only about fifteen per cent of its SSBNs at sea must mean that, in theory, it is vulnerable to ASW operations involving this very localised kind of attack. The Soviet Navy may regard its bases as vulnerable to air attack by long-range missiles or missiles launched from aircraft. In addition, Soviet and other SSBNs are at least potentially vulnerable to offensive mining across base exits or narrow passages through which they must pass to reach their patrol areas.

CONCLUSIONS

The conduct of the strategic strike mission at sea, together with activities intended either to guard forces charged with this role or to attack those of the adversary, are quite clearly a complex and multi-facetted business. The strategic strike equation has many technical and tactical variables. Over the past several decades, technology has

THE IKARA MISSILE

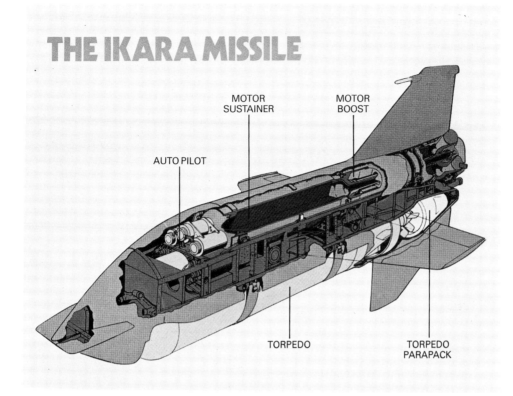

MOTOR
SUSTAINER

MOTOR
BOOST

AUTO PILOT

TORPEDO

TORPEDO
PARAPACK

PLATE 6.7 The *Ikara* anti-submarine missile system allows a surface ship to fire a missile at a detected submarine which then delivers a homing torpedo into its vicinity. (Australian Dept of Defence)

wrought transformations in many of these variables, with effects that ripple through the whole equation and greatly influence the final outcome.

There is little reason to suppose that this process has in any way ended, and the future effects of technological change could easily prove to be as important to the future of this mission, as they have to its past. There are perhaps six areas where change either has had or could have enormous implications.

Nuclear propulsion has transformed the conduct of this role because, when applied to submarines, it has enormously increased the endurance of the primary platform responsible for the task, and at the same time has greatly reduced its visibility.

Long-range SLBMs have proved important either in extending the sea area in which the SSBN can hide, or of making it hardly necessary for the SSBN to leave home waters. Further increases in range might improve this situation marginally, as might the capacity to launch from greater depths, improved communication systems, and an ability to launch SLBMs more rapidly. More capable SLBMs (as measured for example by increased accuracy and/or ability to penetrate enemy defences) have already had important consequences for their targetting potential and may continue to do so. All the same, the distinctive thing about SSBNs is their value as a secure means of retaliation. Regardless of any possible advance in the quality of their missiles, this is likely to continue. *Evasion techniques*, such as the great effort to quieten submarines, are the obvious counter to improved means of detection, and considerable progress in

PLATE 6.8 An *Ikara* missile is launched from a warship of the Royal Australian Navy. (Australian Dept of Defence)

this regard is likely. It is also possible that the submarine's capacity for self-defence, either by being better able to deal with hostile missiles fired at it, or indeed by such things as anti-aircraft missiles fired from underwater, would also increase the SSBNs survivability.

Sonar improvements have so far been the main avenue by which scientists have tried, in the famous phrase, 'to render the oceans transparent'. The balance between the submarine's capacity to hide and the hunter's ability to find it has been largely determined by the current state of sonar technology. There is a widespread view that in the future, active rather than passive sonar will become more important in this regard. If ever the oceans were rendered transparent, the consequences for the conduct of both the strategic deterrence mission and of ASW operations would be quite profound.

Other possibilities. As long ago as 1972, in an article in the Russian journal *Krasnaya Zvezda*, Marshal A. A. Grechko spoke of Soviet interest in such other possibilities as 'infrared, laser, radar, magnetic, gas analysis, radiation, wave detection and even psychic detection'. Certainly other such possibilities exist although they have not so far shown much sign of providing the ASW 'break-through' for which scientists have been looking, but they may yet. There is some interest these days in the detection possibilities of bio-luminescence (the little understood phenomenon by which micro-organisms in the water change colour after large objects have passed through them) and synthetic aperture radar (a satellite based method of plotting the shape of the sea bed by measuring the shape of waves). At the moment, however, most scientists believe that these alternatives will find it difficult to match the performance of contemporary sonar let alone to surpass it.

Strategic Defence. There is considerable interest in the technological prospect of defence against all forms of strategic nuclear attack by dealing not so much with the launching platforms, that is the submarines, but rather by destroying the missiles they launch. This after all is the main idea behind President Reagan's Strategic Defence Initiative. Should anything come of this the consequences could again be quite profound. At the least it could lead to a transformation in the way such attacks are planned; for example, by more widespread use of low-flying cruise missiles, by firing SLBMs close by the enemy on depressed trajectories, by large scale increases in the number of SLBMs and by radical improvements to their intrinsic penetration capability.

7

Operations Against the Shore

A RECAP ON TRADITIONAL THINKING

When they considered the conduct of amphibious operations, the strategists of the machine age came to a number of conclusions which can be boiled down essentially to three points:

(1).   Although there have been exceptions, such as the German invasion of Norway in 1940, navies conducting large scale amphibious operations have generally tried to win high levels of sea control first. The capacity to use the sea as a medium from which to project power ashore, therefore, is generally regarded as one of the main benefits of having command of the sea.

(2).   Amphibious operations come in many different shapes and forms. They may be small scale ones of the sort widely used by the Soviet Navy in World War II. These were intended primarily to aid an advancing or retreating army by using the sea as a way of putting small disruptive forces behind the enemy's front line. Being tactical in intention and responsive to the flow of the land battle they need to be improvised. According to some accounts, sixty-one of the 113 amphibious assaults conducted by the Soviet Navy in the war, were organised the day before! Alternatively, they may be medium sized operations intended to exert a decisive influence on the outcome of a particular campaign. The Soviet operation against Kerch-Feodosiya in 1943 or the Anglo-American Anzio landings of 1944 come into this category. Finally, they may be conducted on a large scale, strategic level where their outcome decisively affects the outcome of the whole war, as was the case in the Normandy landings of 1944, for example.

But on whatever scale they are conducted, operations against the shore are of considerable importance in that they are one of the main means by which maritime powers can help decide the outcome of war on land. The ability to strike against a hostile shore from an unexpected or advantageous direction provides a flexibility which is one of the greatest strategic assets that a maritime power can have. Without it, the value of sea power would be much reduced.

(3).   Nonetheless, amphibious operations are generally agreed to be amongst the most hazardous and difficult operations of war there are. This is because they require high levels of interservice cooperation; moreover they usually rely on the assembly of large numbers of slow and vulnerable ships, packed with people, petrol and ammunition in dangerous places. The bigger the scale of the operation, the higher the extent to which the enemy contests it and the further the landing area from the place where the operation is launched, the more

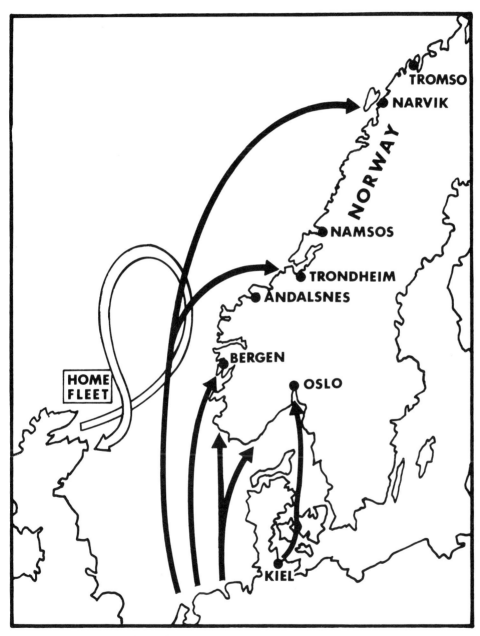

FIG 7.1 The Norway Campaign of 1940 saw one of the most daring amphibious campaigns of the Second World War when, in the presence of superior British naval forces and relying heavily on surprise, German forces made landings at six widely separated points on the coast ranging from Oslo to Narvik.

hazardous it is. All this explains why reasonable levels of sea control are generally regarded as a prerequisite to operations against the shore.

CURRENT DIFFICULTIES

Since 1945, changing technology has confronted amphibious operations with two very serious challenges, which have led many to question their continued validity:

Are They Important? Many experts have argued, as we have seen already, that with the arrival of nuclear weapons, wars between major powers will be short, either because nuclear weapons would be used, or through fear that they might be used unless any war was kept short. Either way, there would probably not be time in most conceivable wars for the lengthy business of organising full-scale amphibious operations, especially if they require the winning of high levels of sea and air control first.

Are They Possible? In an age of missiles and nuclear weapons, the intrinsic vulnerability of amphibious forces to preemptive attack would seem to be hugely increased. After watching the atomic weapon test at Bikini Atoll in 1946, Lieutenant-General Roy S. Geiger (an appropriate name!) of the US Marine Corps, gloomily remarked:

'A small number of atomic bombs could destroy an expeditionary force as now organised, embarked and landed . . . With an enemy in possession of atomic bombs, I cannot visualise another landing such as was executed at Normandy or Okinawa.'

But improvements, even in conventional weaponry, could have the same results. Land-based airpower, modern mines or even missiles fired from shore could have a devastating effect upon the conduct of amphibious operations. There is another problem too. Modern armies around the world have become increasingly mechanised, but the exigencies of having to operate from ships makes it difficult for Marines to keep up with this. Increasingly, they are faced with the choice of resigning themselves to being a 'light' force, which cannot really take on heavy shore based forces in direct combat, or they become a 'heavy' force which has to sacrifice the mobility and flexibility that has been their particular rationale in the past.

Such issues have meant that the postwar careers of the Marine forces of the two Superpowers has been, to say the least, chequered. In the case of the Soviet Naval Infantry, modern scepticism even led to the disbandment of the whole force, and it was only resurrected in 1964.

Despite its great success in World War II, and an impressive performance during the Korean War, the United States Marine Corps (USMC) has been through some vicissitudes too, with some uncertainties about its role. Several options have emerged:

—The USMC should continue to stress preparedness for large scale contested assaults with forces designed to create mass through the provision of very large numbers of men, supported by crushing gunfire and air support against enemy beach defences and air bases.

—The USMC should be regarded primarily as a light force always on patrol with the fleet and ready to be inserted anywhere at a moment's notice. It is *par excellence* the force for sea-based military intervention and diplomatic display, especially in the Third World. In war time it would be a source of rapid reinforcement and of tactical support to the Army, rather in the Soviet style, but on a much bigger scale.

—The USMC should maintain its military skills on the battlefield by fighting alongside conventional army units, as indeed it generally did during the Vietnam War. For this reason, it should acquire the equipment and skills of ordinary army units operating ashore.

This uncertainty and anxiety about the implications of technology for the whole rationale of the USMC led to doubts about its continued survival. This scepticism reached the highest levels. In 1975, James Schlesinger, Secretary of Defense remarked:

> An amphibious assault force . . . has not seen anything more demanding than essentially unopposed landings for over twenty years, and . . . would have grave difficulties in accomplishing the mission of over-the-beach and flanking operations in a high-threat environment.

At this time quite a few people believed that the USMC stood in immediate danger of degenerating into an under-gunned, slow-moving monument to a bygone era in warfare.

TECHNOLOGY TO THE RESCUE

Coping with Nuclear Weapons

This subject has been explored with some rigour by Soviet writers. The extent to which amphibious operations have been practised in exercises suggest that they, at least, have few doubts about the continued necessity for operations against the shore, even in the context of a major East-West war in Europe. The continued importance of the task would not appear to be in doubt—in the Soviet Union at any rate!

The difficulties associated with the conduct of such operations in the face of an adversary armed with nuclear weapons is, however, admitted by Soviet commentators. Nuclear weapons could have a very considerable effect on forces attempting large-scale amphibious landings. In response, three points are often made:

—The dangers of nuclear attack can be mitigated by a number of palliatives, such as making the best possible use of strategic surprise, of deception and of dispersing forces amongst a large number of fast moving platforms.

—All military operations in a nuclear environment, ashore as well as at sea, will likely be much more dispersed, fluid and decentralised than usual. This lack of operational density makes the enemy's rear areas particularly susceptible to assaults from the sea.

—Amphibious forces can use nuclear weapons too, and this might be a very good way of suppressing landward defences before the amphibious assault goes in.

Soviet amphibious exercises are often conducted in a simulated nuclear environment, sometimes with the shore defender using them and sometimes the sea-based attacker. In Okean-1970, for instance, landings in the Baltic area were only started after the defender had suffered a nuclear bombardment. The same thing happened at more or less the same time in an assault on the Rybachii peninsula near Murmansk, with the nuclear fire-support evidently being provided by submarines.

This argument, of course, is not to say that amphibious operations conducted in a nuclear environment would be unaffected by that fact. It suggests merely that it is not clear that they would suffer proportionately more than other military or indeed civilian activities.

PLATE 7.1 Soviet Naval Infantry in action. Soviet amphibious warfare is more localised and tactical than its Western counterpart, although its capacity is steadily growing. (Tass Photo)

Coping With Air Attack

Modern conventional munitions too pose a considerable threat to large concentrations of slow-moving ships full of troops and costly, often highly flammable, material. Three responses to this have been proposed:

—Dispersion, surprise and deception, as was the case for coping with nuclear weapons.

—Organic airpower is the answer to shore-based air attack as much now as it was in World War II. The problem of making sure that there would be enough aircraft present to conduct this supportive mission has been greatly aided by the development of VSTOL aircraft like the *Harrier*. It is no coincidence that it was the USMC, above all others, who were interested in developing this revolutionary type of aircraft, because its operating characteristics fitted their requirements exactly.

PLATE 7.2 The US Marine Corps has always been enthusiastic about the possibilities of VSTOL aircraft as a means of providing amphibious forces with air support. The AV-8B is an American development of the Harrier concept. (British Aerospace)

Airpower in another form also helps amphibious forces cope with the challenges posed by modern defensive weaponry. The use of helicopters as a means of troop transport and gunfire support makes 'vertical envelopment' possible. The speed of this type of attack will minimise the vulnerability of the landing force and offers good prospects, its adherents claim, of overwhelming local defences.

—Indeed, speed is the answer to the problem of vulnerability in many other ways too. The Soviet Naval Infantry, for example, puts great stress on the value of hovercraft in the amphibious role. They are both fast, and flexible because they can cross land, sea and the marginal areas in between with equal facility. New technology, in this case, appears to be at least a partial answer to the problems that other sorts of new technology create.

PLATE 7.3 The CH-53 *Sea Stallion* is important to the US Marine Corps' concept of vertical envelopment. It has a cruising speed of 150 knots, a combat radius of 100 nautical miles and can carry thirty-seven combat ready marines or a load of 8000 pounds. (USMC)

CONCEPT ATTENUATION

This is no more than a way of saying that, in response to the conditions imposed by new technology, it may be necessary to water the basic idea of amphibious operations down a little, while preserving most of their essential character.

Attenuation of Means. One way of reducing the specification for amphibious forces is to say that they could make do with less demanding equipment. Bearing in mind the high costs, brought about by their technological sophistication, or purpose-built amphibious shipping, the question arises: could they not employ converted or adapted civilian shipping instead? After all, the development of modularisation, discussed earlier, means that North Sea ferries, for example, could be quite effective in this role, as the Falklands conflict showed.

Marines of all nationalities tend to resist such arguments and stress the need for specialist amphibious shipping since this is the optimum way of providing necessary command-and-control, air support, logistics back-up and so forth. Mindful of the Soviet Navy's special experience of this expedient during World War II, Admiral Stalbo has pointed out: 'The lack of specialised landing ships often led to considerable losses of landing forces and made weather conditions of special significance.'

Nevertheless, the possibility of making do with less (perhaps as exemplified

PLATE 7.4 HMS *Fearless* seen off the coast of Norway. Specialist amphibious warfare ships of this sort are valuable in that they provide command and control facilities, good helicopter support, supplies and a floodable dock at the stern for landing craft. (MOD (Navy))

by the *Harrier*) continues to attract interest, at least as an alternative to making do with nothing at all.

Attenuation of Ends. Here the idea is to preserve the amphibious warfare mission in the face of the new challenges it faces by emphasising the feasibility and attractiveness of its less ambitious forms. Rather than stress the Normandy alternative mentioned above, preference is given instead to intervention capabilities in the Third World and in a major war to light and localised amphibious operations.

Typical of this stress, for example would be the role of the Dutch and British amphibious landing force which, in the event of hostilities on NATO's Northern Flank, are expected to be an important part of the allies reinforcement response. As described by a recent Commandant General of the Royal Marines, Lieutenant General Sir Steuart Pringle, a force like this, if supported by a minimum of specialised equipment, offers both in peace and in war more or less unlimited mobility and ability to advance, withdraw, concentrate or disperse without violating frontiers or abandoning ground. This capacity is the product of six characteristics, he has said:

—It can be deployed without commitment, and be held poised, giving any one of a wide range of possible political signals to potential enemies.

—It can divert *en route* to the theatre of operations, if circumstances ashore so dictate, and be held in reserve or be deployed to an entirely different area.

— It can provide a graduated response, depending on the operational circumstances, ranging from rapid deployment ashore of the whole force, to withdrawal without commitment.

—It can provide tactical surprise by landing where the enemy is not.

—It is structured to land in a combat posture and fight on arrival.

—Once ashore, the whole or part of the force can be re-embarked and redeployed.

PLATE 7.5 Amphibious warfare may range from large full-scale amphibious landings to small raids of the type pictured here. (MOD (Navy))

PLATE 7.6 Amphibious warfare demands a great deal of specialised equipment and training.
Here a group of Dutch Marines, together with some of their vehicles, head for the shore of a
Norwegian fjord on a mexifloat. (MOD (Navy))

PLATE 7.7 Many of the world's navies maintain a capacity for small scale amphibious
operations and retain a number of small amphibious warfare craft for the purpose. *Zander*
is one of the 520 class of small landing craft maintained by the West German Navy. *Zander* is
166 tons standard and 403 tons full load displacement.

It is important to note that however impressive this seems, it is no Normandy option that has been described above, in that such an amphibious force is not expected to land in the presence of strong enemy forces (and would have to be considerably strengthened in every particular if it was preparing for direct operations against heavy Soviet ground forces, for example). Moreover, once ashore, a light amphibious force would not be equipped to do more than to harass and hinder an approaching mechanised or armoured division; in normal circumstances engaging such an adversary in direct combat would be most unwise. That is not its role.

THE FALKLANDS EXAMPLE

Many of these characteristics were well demonstrated in the Falklands conflict of 1982. The original Argentine operation against the Falklands and South Georgia, and the British counter-operation against South Georgia were perhaps relatively minor examples of the *genre* but the final British operation at San Carlos was a much larger scale affair. Indeed, the biggest in scale since the Inchon landings of 1950, the Suez operation of 1956 or the Turkish invasion of Cyprus in 1974.

Complicated by the great range at which the operation was conducted, the Task Force went through all the normal preliminaries and preparations and then conducted a standard, indeed almost textbook, landing operation. The stages, roughly, were:

Preparation. Everything the Task Force needed had to be taken with it,

PLATE 7.8 Landing craft from HMS *Fearless* approach the shore of San Carlos Water during the Falklands campaign. (MOD (Navy))

transported and packed in battle order, with due allowance made for losses and enemy action.

Sea and Air Control. To the extent necessary, though not to the extent the British desired, air and sea superiority was won both before and during the operation to allow it to proceed.

PLATE 7.9 *Sea Harriers* proved in the Falklands campaign to be effective in providing the amphibious operations area with a reasonable degree of air cover. (MOD (Navy))

Reconnaissance of possible landing sites was conducted by helicopter, submarine and by small detachments of special forces put ashore for the purpose.

Deception and Surprise. Every effort was made to distract and confuse the enemy by feints, diversionary raids and shore bombardments.

The Landing Operation was successfully conducted in the face of slight enemy opposition.

Combat with Main Forces Ashore. Once landed and sorted out, the landing force advanced overland to engage the enemy's main military formations ashore.

Logistic support. Once again, the tremendous consumption rates of modern warfare were demonstrated. Forces ashore had constantly to be restocked with everything they needed to continue military operations.

Air Cover. An early seizure and subsequent exploitation of air bases ashore was not possible in this case, so the Task Force had to continue to provide air support throughout the operation.

Supplementary Landings. The subsequent progress of the main forces ashore were much aided by the staging of tactical landings behind the forward edge of the battle area.

Naval Gunfire Support by warships operating offshore proved to be extremely effective, despite years of scepticism in the West.

PLATE 7.10 Naval gunfire support was also found to be much more effective than commonly thought. The 4.5″ guns of British frigates, pictured here firing on Argentine positions in South Georgia, proved to be fast and accurate. (MOD (Navy))

The Falklands landing operation was on a smaller scale than the large amphibious operations conducted during World War II but in all other respects was remarkably similar. This indicates the extent to which the challenge of new technology has been contained, and indeed exploited by the practitioners of this form of maritime warfare.

PLATE 7.11 Naval gunfire support of a completely different sort. Here the 16″ guns of the battleship USS *Iowa* are fired in support of a recent USMC exercise in Korea. (US Navy)

PLATE 7.12 Crewmen wheeling the massive power casing (the cartridge, not the shell) of one of the USS *New Jersey*'s 16" guns. The projectile itself weighs 2700 lb and can be fired up to 23 miles. (US Navy)

SOVIET EXPERIENCE

While no amphibious operation is 'typical', Operation Corporate was in many ways a textbook example of its kind. Nevertheless, it is worth comparing it briefly with standard Soviet amphibious operations, just to demonstrate the variety of forms this type of sea warfare can take.

There seem to be four main differences:

(1). *The Waiting and Embarkation Area.* Soviet thinking stresses the importance of the waiting area, ie the place where the amphibious assault force prepares itself for the action, and the embarkation area where it goes to sea. It is important to protect this area against enemy air action, especially as it will usually be within one night's steaming of its intending landing place. Normal 'tactical' Soviet operations would involve a landing force of up to 10,000.

(2). *Defence of the Sea Passage.* Because Soviet amphibious operations normally take place in close proximity to the battle front, strong enemy counteraction must be prepared for. Air defence will be provided by land-based aircraft. An area support group of large ships (destroyers, frigates and helicopter carriers), sailing perhaps thirty kilometres from the assault force, will protect it from enemy surface attack, submarines and aircraft. A close ASW force will screen it from submarines, and to an extent from fast attack craft.

The assault force itself will sail in multiple columns, and will include assault ships, tugs, rescue ships, freighters, storeships and so on. The ships will sail between 500 and 5000 metres behind the one ahead with others about 1000–6000 metres on either side. The greater the likelihood of nuclear attack, the larger the distances observed.

(3). *Preparation of Assault Landing Area.* A mine counter-measures force will sweep the landing area for mines, while fast attack craft will land frogmen and others to dash ashore to blow up obstacles and so forth. Local land-based fighters will seek to establish command of the air and bombers will exploit this by beginning an intense air bombardment of the area. Attention is paid during this phase to the need to avoid showing the enemy exactly where the landing will take place.

(4). *The Landing Operation.* Localised air strikes will increase in intensity, and land-based artillery will usually join in too (another reminder of how close these operations normally are to the forward edge of the battle area). Parachutists will be deployed and ships at sea will open fire on important strongpoints, enemy formations and so on. All of these will depend on intelligence provided by reconnaissance forces landed during the preparatory phase.

The first wave of the assault forces will try to land tanks and infantry straight onto the shore but if this is not possible, amphibious tanks and armoured personnel carriers will disembark into the water to lead the assault. This is the particular role of the Soviet Naval Infantry. Unless enemy resistance is heavy, all these vehicles will drive ashore and go on to attack their objectives. If the enemy resistance is strong, troops will dismount to fight their way ashore.

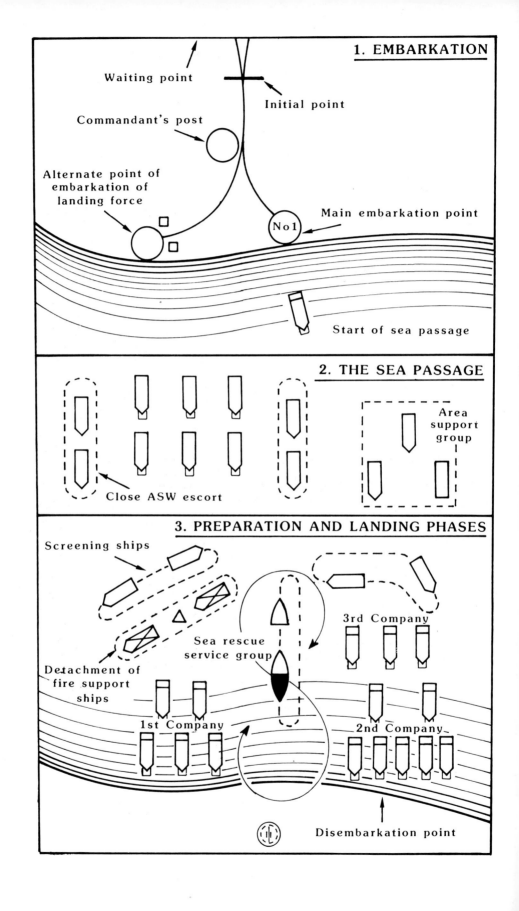

1. EMBARKATION

Waiting point

Initial point

Commandant's post

Alternate point of embarkation of landing force

Main embarkation point

No 1

Start of sea passage

2. THE SEA PASSAGE

Area support group

Close ASW escort

3. PREPARATION AND LANDING PHASES

Screening ships

3rd Company

Sea rescue service group

Detachment of fire support ships

1st Company

2nd Company

Disembarkation point

PLATE 7.13 The Soviet *Ivan Rogov* amphibious warfare ship of 11,000 tons standard displacement. One of the most effective units in the Soviet amphibious fleet, this ship has helicopter landing decks fore and aft, and can accommodate about 550 troops with all their equipment including twenty tanks. The stern dock carries 3 ACVs. (MOD (Navy))

FIG 7.2 (*opposite*) The Main Stages of a Soviet Amphibious Assault, in Battalion Strength. Source: C Donnelly *et al.*, *Soviet Amphibious Warfare*, Soviet Studies Centre, Sandhurst, 1985.

PLATE 7.14 For comparison, another 11,000 ton amphibious warfare ship, HMS *Fearless*. The two landing craft dimly visible in the dock show why this class of ship is known as a Landing Platform Dock (LPD). Large ships like the *Ivan Rogov* and *Fearless* can stay at sea for long periods and afford a commander considerable operational flexibility. (MOD (Navy))

About fifteen minutes later, the second wave will appear, bringing with them main battle tanks, air defence weapons, anti-tank guns, communications and engineering equipment, and NBC support if necessary. Already operations will begin to assume the character of normal ground force battle.

The most obvious differences between this and the Falklands example, is the proximity of the embarkation and landing areas and the consequent need for very extensive supporting operations.

DEFENCE AGAINST AMPHIBIOUS OPERATIONS

The continued viability of amphibious operations in the nuclear age is further confirmed by the attention that many of the world's navies pay to defeating them. The defence policies of countries like Denmark and Norway, for example, are heavily affected by the need to guard the coastline against such operations.

But perhaps the country which pays most attention to this need is their most obvious possible adversary, the Soviet Union, which has always given a great deal of precedence to the defence of the homeland against sea-based attack and continues to do so.

Broadly speaking, the Soviet solution to the problem appears to be to establish a defensive system comprising a series of concentric arcs centred on vulnerable parts of the Soviet Union like the Kola peninsula. These arcs comprise bands of different

PLATE 7.15 The West German Navy's shore based *Tornado* force is an important part of NATO's defence of Schleswig-Holstein, Jutland and the Danish Islands from the threat of amphibious attack. (FGN)

PLATE 7.16 The SSMs and 76 mm gun of this *Albatross* class of FAC in service with the West Germany Navy are also ideally suited to the defence of such areas against amphibious attack, because their speed and small size means they can make the best use of broken coastlines and narrow seas. (FGN)

defensive forces. The homeland defence exercise of 1983 showed the concept well. As the simulated carrier/invasion forces approached the Soviet Union, they were engaged by torpedo and cruise missile firing submarines, then by shore-based aircraft. If these forces had survived to sail further north, they would then also have been engaged by large surface warships operating in specific task groups, and finally by a large offshore defence force comprising small missile firing warships like the *Osa* and *Nanuchka*. In short, the closer an adversary approaches the Soviet Union, the thicker and more diverse the maritime defences.

In the Soviet case, technology has affected the execution of this task in a number of ways:

—It has considerably affected *the nature of the perceived threat*. In the early days, the threat was seen to be standard amphibious forces of the sort so well employed by the West in World War II. In the 1950s and 1960s, carrier battle groups were added to the cast of possible adversaries. Since then, land-attack cruise missiles have attracted a good deal of Soviet attention.

—Technology has greatly extended *the depth of the defences*. Stalin's navy could hope to create a defensive system of some 500 miles. Nowadays the outer edge of this defensive system, its submarine line, extends to the south of Ireland. The inclusion of an increasing part of Western Europe, and of the Far East inside the defensive perimeter of the Soviet Union, could be politically and strategically very significant.

—Technology has sometimes provided the Soviet Union with an *alternative response* to a perceived threat it could not hope to counter directly. For example, the clear American lead in the deployment of carrier battle groups could not be answered by the creation of Soviet equivalents. Instead, the Soviet Union sought to outflank its adversary by developing the alternative of long-

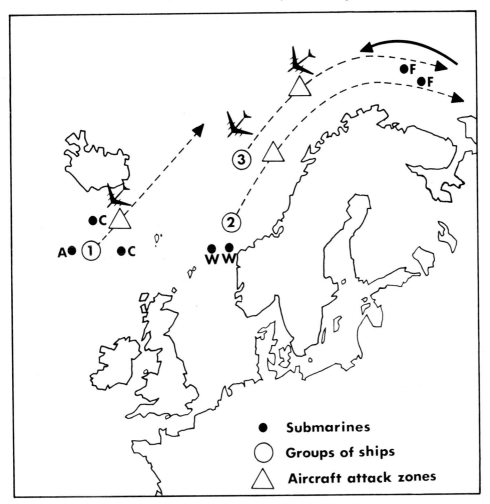

FIG 7.3 The Soviet Homeland Defence Exercise of Autumn 1983. In this exercise simulated carrier battle groups comprising the Soviet carrier *Novorossisk* plus supporting ships, and possibly amphibious warfare groups were attacked by *Alpha* torpedo firing (A) and *Charlie* missile firing submarines (C). Older *Whiskey* (W) and *Foxtrot* (F) submarines were also in attendance. Incoming forces were subjected to attack by increasingly heavy waves of land-based aircraft. Waiting for the survivors to the north of Norway were mission oriented anti-submarine and anti-surface ship task groups. (Source: US DOD)

range naval missiles fired from shore based aircraft, submarines and surface warships.

—*The orchestrated multidimensional attack* is one of the most obvious hallmarks of Soviet naval operations. By using large number of different platforms and weapons, as we have already seen, the Soviet Navy hopes to overwhelm the adversary by the weight, diversity and simultaneity of its attack. In so far as it contributes to this diversity of response, technology may be said to help the execution of this task. On the other hand, it adds diversity to the invader's means of attack too.

—Finally, technology makes this defensive system transportable because it is based, at least to some extent, on mobile rather than fixed platforms. This means *the extension of the system* to areas other than around the Soviet Union is easier. Nowadays, allies of the Soviet Union in distant areas might also expect protection against amphibious attack.

The frequency with which the Soviet Union and other countries conduct exercises in which they defend themselves against amphibious assaults of various kinds is strong evidence of the continuing effectiveness of this function of sea power in the nuclear age, earlier scepticism notwithstanding.

CONCLUSIONS

Partly with the aid of the three saving graces described above, amphibious warfare has evidently survived as a significant element of modern warfare at sea. Minor and/or supportive landings, uncontested or conducted in the presence of only limited opposition, have in fact been a relatively common element of maritime operations since 1945. And there have been a few larger examples of the *genre* too.

Both the Superpowers maintain, despite the difficulties, large amphibious forces and to judge by their construction and support plans, appear convinced that this method of warfare has a secure future.

8

Maritime Interdiction

THE IMPORTANCE OF SEA TRADE

As Admiral Moineville reminds us:

> The merchant vessel, has been, since the dawn of civilisation, an essential agent of commerce, barter and consequently of development; and its role continues to grow alongside that of the aeroplane. For example, from 1964 to 1979, the tonnage of the world's merchant fleets increased from 137 to 393 million tons gross. This expansion itself shows how the dependence of nations on maritime transport has increased. The merchant vessel has two essential virtues—its great capacity and its low cost per ton-kilometre—which hold to fundamental physical laws and assure its remaining the prime means of transport for the forseeable future. The attack and defence of maritime transport will therefore remain at the heart of naval warfare.

Since 1945 world trade has increased eightfold and is set to grow further as the world's population grows and economic interdependence between countries expands. National self-sufficiency is rapidly becoming a thing of the past. A large proportion of this trade is conducted by merchant ship and the present volume of international seaborne trade is around 3200 million tonnes a year (nearly forty per cent of which is oil). The average distance at which seaborne trade is conducted is now 4200 nautical miles. In these circumstances, the overwhelming importance of merchant shipping to the world economy is hardly a matter of dispute.

In a general sense, as we have already seen, sea power has always comprised two separate but closely connected elements, namely the merchant fleet and the military fleet. Because the merchant fleet is such a valuable asset, its defence at sea has been a high priority for navies. Moreover, some of the characteristics of a strong merchant fleet (particularly hulls, trained seamen, sea-based wealth and a general sense of the importance of the sea to the nation) have made an important contribution to naval power. For such reasons, these two elements of sea power have tended to rise and fall together.

Some qualifications should perhaps be entered against this general proposition, however. There are, and always have been exceptions to the general rule. Japan, Greece and Norway all maintain large merchant fleets but do not deploy the kind of navy that can offer them much assistance, especially if they are away from home. Moreover, the protection of the merchant fleet is, as we have seen, far from being the only purpose for which navies are created. There would still be a need for naval power if all the merchant fleets of the world were swept from the ocean.

Nevertheless, generally speaking, the two elements tend to go hand in hand. The connected rise to prominence of the merchant and naval fleets of the Soviet Union since the 1950s is only the most obvious recent example of the phenomenon. Currently the merchant fleet of the Soviet Bloc is as follows:

TABLE 8.1 *The Soviet Bloc Merchant Fleet*
(as at 30th June in each year)

	1983		1985		1986	
	Number	GRT	Number	GRT	Number	GRT
Totals over 100 GRT (all types)	9,597	33.6	8,785	32.8	8,551	34.8
excluding Albania, Cuba, Yugoslavia:			922	3.7	932	4.3
including Trading Vessels	3,736	24.6	3,573	25.3	3,490	25.7
also—Fishing Vessels over 100 GRT*	4,981	7.8	4,209	7.5	3,903	7.6
inc. over 500 GRT*			2,676	3.5		
Offshore Support Vessels	31	0.03	63	0.04	70	0.041
Research & Intelligence*	184	0.34	190	0.34	190	0.25
Icebreakers*	43	0.24	35	0.22	40	0.25

*Largest Fleets of their types in the world (but fish catch only 2nd after Japan).
For Comparison:
Japan is the largest national-flag fleet, i.e. not a 'flag of convenience':

	1983		1985		1986	
including:			10,288	40.0	10,011	38.5
2nd largest fishing fleet	3,003	1.1	2,917	1.0	2,828	1.1
but only over 500 GRT		0.36	147	0.39		
WORLD	76,106	422.6	76,395	416.3	75,266	404.9
including Trading Vessels	40,665	399.6	40,217	392.5	39,200	381.0

All above figures from Lloyd's Register of Shipping Statistical Tables for year concerned; GRT in million tons.
(*Source: British Maritime League Memorandum 'The Decline of the UK Registered Merchant Fleet'.*)

As the Soviet merchant and fishing fleets grow in size and economic importance, there will no doubt develop perceived vulnerabilities and the Soviet Navy will be charged with its defence. In fact this development is already underway. Admiral Gorshkov has noted that however ancient this task might be it retains its importance 'even in present day conditions'. Moreover, 'with the growth of the economic power of the Soviet Union, its interests on the seas and oceans are expanding to an even greater degree and consequently new requirements are laid on the Navy to defend them from Imperialist encroachments'.

THE SPECTRUM OF THREAT

Both in peace and war, so valuable an asset is likely to come under a variety of threats.

The Economic Threat

This is perhaps the most serious threat and it is one about which naval power can do very little. Taking the British as a particularly bad, but by no means unique, example of the case, there has been a drastic decline in the size of the merchant fleet. Whereas, in 1974 the British merchant fleet stood at over 1900 ships at some 47.8 million deadweight tons (when the British merchant fleet was the world's second largest), by the mid 1980s it had fallen to just over a quarter of this total. It is by no means clear, yet, that this trend has bottomed out either. The consequences are clear:

—The percentage of British import and export trade carried by British ships has fallen drastically. In 1975, about fifty-seven per cent of British exports and thirty-four per cent of imports were carried in British ships; ten years later, this had dropped to eighteen per cent and twenty-three per cent respectively.
—The nett contribution made by British-owned ships to the overall balance of payments has also fallen. In 1975 this contribution approached £3,000 million a year, but ten years later it was only £750 million.
—There has also been a sharp fall in the general maritime infrastructure. Ship-building and ship-repair have both declined. British yards completed about 550,000 gross registered tonnage in 1975, but less than half that a decade later. In 1975, Britain had about 100,000 qualified sea-farers, but hardly a third of that total in 1985.

And so the dismal catalogue goes on. Britain, being a particularly maritime nation, tends to feel the draught more than most countries do, but it is, to a greater or lesser degree, a widespread phenomenon. Norway, Sweden, Finland and all the countries of the European Community are suffering in the same way. The Socialist countries of Eastern Europe have more ships now than they had in 1975, but still have a reduced percentage of world shipping; the same thing applies to the merchant fleets of Flags of Convenience states, most of which are actually owned, of course, by Western concerns.

The one exception to this, is the growth in the size, and the proportion of the fleets of Asia. Hong Kong, India, Pakistan, Korea, Singapore and Taiwan, in particular, show strong growth in the size of their merchant fleet, and in the maritime infrastructure. China too is turning into a considerable power at sea. Japan's growth in comparison is relatively modest.

Reasons for the Decline

How is this general decline to be explained? A number of factors account for it, although the extent of their application varies widely from country to country as we have seen. A good many of these basic causes are a consequence of new technology, directly or indirectly. Amongst these causes, and in no particular priority there are the following:

—The special decline of the merchant fleets of the Atlantic countries can be seen as just another example of important basic shifts in the world economy, many of which give greater prominence to the countries of the Pacific Rim.
—Some countries have had greater success than others in compensating for the increased cost of modern shipping technology, by reducing their labour, insurance, infrastructure and financial management costs.
—There is a good deal of overcapacity. The world merchant fleet currently comprises some 40,000 trading vessels, of which 27,000 are over 500 gross registered tons. According to some estimates, this is nearly twice the fleet actually needed for dealing with the present volume of world trade.

—Technology has made other forms of carriage available, including oil pipelines, the Trans-Siberian Railway, air transport and so on which offer competitive alternatives.

—There is a good deal of over-production of new ships. In 1985 total world shipbuilding output totalled 18.2 gross registered tons of which 52.3 per cent came from Japan, with the other Asian countries adding another seventeen per cent. Western Europe and the United States together provided a further 17.6 per cent.

—Modern ship technology means ships carry larger cargoes, and so fewer are needed. Efficient container ships, very large tankers and bulk cargo ships considerably reduce the need for ship numbers. One 300,000 ton supertanker may easily replace eight or more small ones.

—There are important differences in the extent to which individual countries support their national merchant fleets. Governmental policies on direct or indirect subsidies, cargo reservation, and even on the extent of regulation may all be important contributory factors to relative success in retaining merchant fleet size.

Military Implications

This decline in national merchant fleets could have quite severe military repercussions, if it went so far as to deprive navies of the ships they need, for example, to transport men and military materials to the battle area. It is generally said that in order to fight a sustained war in Western Europe, NATO would need about 800 reinforcement/resupply ship loads across the Atlantic in the first month and about 600 per month after that. The war economy of Western Europe would need a further 1500 ship-loads a month. Obviously, if the over-all NATO shipping pool, which is currently about 6000 ships, fell so low as to make it difficult to get the numbers of ships that reinforcement required, the military implications could be very severe. At the moment, the consensus view is that NATO does have the shipping it needs in overall terms but a continuation of present trends could threaten this.

There are, needless to say, many complicating factors. Assumed loss rates (which could easily be twenty-five per cent in the first month, declining thereafter) need to be taken into the overall equation, as does the requirement to move people and materials around inside Europe, as well as across the Atlantic. While the overall shipping availability figure may be acceptable, this may nevertheless conceal shortages in certain types of shipping.

It is also true that the commercial pressures on merchant shipping push shipowners in directions which are sometimes militarily disadvantageous. For example, the modern trend toward container ships may not be militarily helpful as they require specialist loading/unloading facilities which may not be available where needed. To save costs, ship-owners also increasingly resort to 'flagging out', that is to making use of flags of convenience; this could lead to legal problems should governments wish to requisition ships in an emergency; complex ownership of ships by multi-national corporations could be a problem too. The employment of cheap personnel from outside NATO could lead to a shortfall of available sea-farers within it.

During the Falklands conflict, the contribution made to a country's sea power by

PLATE 8.1 This picture of part of Kiel docks shows two things. Firstly the line of merchant vessels illustrate the growing economic importance of the merchant fleet. Secondly the Soviet ship in the centre shows how merchant hulls can be converted to a variety of civilian and/or military purposes. Originally built as a timber carrier, the *Borovichi* now carries the variety of tracking, direction-finding and directional antennae typical of a ship used in the Soviet space research programme.

its merchant marine and its supporting infrastructure was convincingly demonstrated. Three large passenger liners, fifteen tankers, eight Ro-Ro general cargo ships, one container ship, one cable ship, five trawlers, four passenger cargo ships, six general cargo ships, four offshore support vessels and four tugs were pressed into service in a whole variety of indispensable roles. Many of these ships had to be fitted for war service with helicopter pads, replenishment-at-sea facilities and so forth. That so many ships were thus converted in a few days and virtually without notice was a considerable tribute to the residual versatility of Britain's ship-building and repair yards. Finally, with the ships sailed some 330 officers and 1170 men of the Merchant Navy. There is considerable justice in the view that were it not for the merchant navy, the Royal Navy might as well have stayed at home. Commercial or other developments that threaten the merchant navy's capacity to act in this way, therefore, could have very serious military implications.

For this reason, many naval experts believe that countries cannot afford to take their merchant fleets for granted. They suggest a number of protective devices. These included maintaining an updated register of currently available shipping, legislation to effect rapid requisitioning when necessary, government subsidies to assure the survival of shipping necessary for strategic purposes, the inclusion of certain military features (like strengthened decks) in new ship-building and so on.

The fact that this issue is taken so seriously that the military as well as the commercial consequences of changes in the world wide merchant shipping industry, many of which are the consequences of various technological developments, could be very important.

Endemic Threats in the Third World

Disorder is endemic in large parts of the Third World and much of this has an impact on the safety of merchant shipping. Piracy is commonplace in parts of South East Asia, and off West Africa too. The recent *Achille Lauro* incident in the Mediterranean is only one of the more obvious manifestations of a trend towards maritime terrorism which is disturbing ship-operators. But the Gulf War between Iran and Iraq shows that the worst threat currently facing merchant shipping in the Third World is of being involved, directly or indirectly, in local wars.

Coherent anti-shipping campaigns have been fought elsewhere too. As an example, we may take the Arab-Israeli War of 1973. The consumption of military supplies meant that both sides had to be provided with large amounts of military equipment during the course of the conflict, mainly by the superpowers. As far as the then Commander-in-Chief of the Israeli Navy, Admiral Benjamin Telem, was concerned, 'The Yom Kippur War has proved to us as well as to the Arabs the great importance of open sea lanes in any all-out conflict.'

Though neither side chose to attack the merchant shipping of the opposition's main ally, the attack and defence of merchant shipping involved them both in a wide range of activities. Defensively, the protagonists sought to protect their shipping by sinking the forces that might threaten it (such as the Israeli destruction at Ghardala on the Red Sea of an Egyptian *Komar* fast patrol boat which had already disrupted Israeli shipping) or by providing direct 'cover'. Merchant ships proceeding to Israel through the Eastern Mediterranean were afforded protection, sometimes by close escort if particular vessels were especially important.

Methods of attack were equally varied. Declaration of military and blockade zones, the existence of ruse, and real, minefields and commercial pressure on neutrals, had important deterrent effects. The blockade established by the Egyptian Navy at Bab-el-Mandeb from 11th October to 13th December was apparently effective; merchant ships were stopped and searched, some were turned back, shot at or sunk. A minefield near the Straits of Tiran reinforced a blockade which effectively choked off Israel's Red Sea traffic, although this, in the midst of a war, was unlikely to be great in any case. Both sides sought to attack each other's shipping in the Mediterranean. The Israelis, for example, attacked the Egyptian fishing fleet and raided such Syrian ports as Tartus and Latakia on several occasions, attacking ships and installations.

It is clear from this survey that merchant shipping operated either by one of the belligerents of a local war, or by a neutral with business in the area, could easily face the whole gamut of technological threats both at sea and in nearby ports. In recent years, merchant ships have been damaged or sunk by mines, gunfire, surface-to-surface missiles, air-to-surface missiles and torpedoes. Such threats, of course, encourage the idea that even distant neutrals may need to consider the protection of their merchant shipping from the consequences of a local war, a rationale frequently

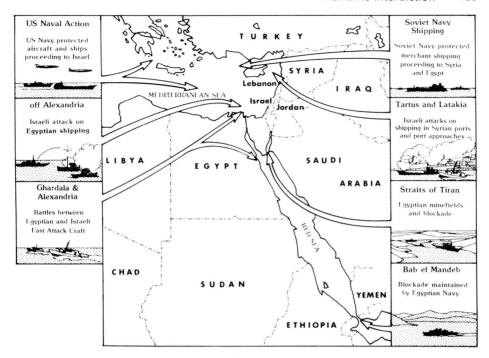

FIG 8.1 Maritime Interdiction in the 1973 Arab-Israeli War.

cited for the presence of British, French and American naval forces in the Gulf and Indian Ocean areas, for example.

There is also the widely canvassed possibility that a great power might seek to advance its interest by harassing the merchant shipping of either a local power or even its great power rival. The first of these situations has certainly happened, and there have even been examples of the latter (off Cuba in 1962, and Nicaragua in 1985) although these were conducted with considerable care and politeness. Prolonged and serious great power harassment of each other's merchant shipping may not seem very likely but it is as well to remember a point made by France's Admiral Moineville: 'It is reasonable to assume that the leaders in a crisis, conscious of the consequences of a nuclear exchange, will seek to exhaust all other possibilities before resorting to it.'

Maritime Interdiction in a Major War

Clearly, the biggest single threat faced by merchant shipping would be that confronted in the course of a major war between NATO and the Warsaw Pact. In many ways, this threat would be the same as that faced by the belligerents in the Arab-Israeli War of 1973, only magnified many times over in terms of the number and diversity of potential targets and of possible assailants. Moreover, the quality of the weaponry deployed for and against the protection of merchant shipping would be substantively different, especially if nuclear weapons were used.

The fact that Western Europe is divided from its main ally, on whose forces it relies for its ultimate security, by the Atlantic Ocean means, at least on the face of it, that merchant shipping will be urgently required for reinforcement and resupply. According to estimates in the German Defence White Paper of 1983, the United States will wish to reinforce the four Divisions already deployed in the country and bring in a further six within the first two weeks of a conflict. More than 100,000 tons of cargo is need to transport one mechanised division, and it will need a further 1000 tons a day to keep going. Without those forces, NATO's defences in Western Europe could easily be faced with the prospect of collapse or of reluctant escalation to nuclear warfare in a rather short space of time. Thus, the normal argument goes, the security of NATO's Sea lines of Communication (SLOCs) would be of paramount importance in a major war against the Soviet Union. That being so, the Soviet Union must seek to attack them; faced with such a campaign, the West must accordingly defend them.

This is not to say, however, that such conventional wisdom is without sceptics. Arguments against this standard justification for the protection of reinforcement/resupply shipping include:

—A war on the Central Front is likely to be short and violent, quite possibly involving the use of nuclear weapons. There would be no time to bring in new soldiers or equipment. Forces not in the battle area on Day 1 might as well stay at home. Reinforcement has to take place *before* the fighting starts, and should be regarded as a deliberate act of deterrence.

—Major industrial nations have sufficient stockpiles to outlast the longest of short wars; or, if they haven't, they should.

—The existence of nuclear weapons, the possibility of heavy attack on ports even with conventional means (including mines) and the sheer time required to organise it means that a significant reinforcement effort is simply not feasible.

—The Soviet Union does not have the forces to make a serious challenge to reinforcement and resupply shipping at sea, especially in view of the other things it needs to do with its Navy, such as protecting its SSBNs and its territory from Western attack.

Many of these are large issues admitting no simple proofs or disproofs, and we have already come across some of them elsewhere in this book. Deciding the length of war for which a naval planner should prepare is about the most difficult issue there is. It involves prediction of future political and military policies and events, estimates of the impact of weapons hardly tried out in anger and, above all, the certainly that a resourceful adversary will respond creatively to whatever one decides to do. Most analysts accept that it would be extremely unwise to neglect the need to protect reinforcement shipping on the basis that the war would be over too quickly for it to matter, on four grounds:

1. Prewar estimates are often wrong.
2. There is a need for reinforcement shipping within the theatre of military operations as well as to it.
3. Such a policy would be a self-fulfilling prophecy because without the necessary reinforcements, NATO would have either to escalate or stop fighting.

4. One side's preparations for a short war are the other side's incentives for a long one.

These are plainly difficult and often controversial matters, and is worth remarking again that they spring in large measure from the new technology of war.

For the remainder of this chapter, we will assume that there is a need to protect merchant shipping and consider briefly how this might be done. While the thrust of the discussion will be largely about maritime interdiction in a serious East-West war, it is clear, as we have already seen, that a good deal of it will apply also to smaller examples of the *genre* in the Third World and elsewhere.

CHANGING TECHNOLOGY AND THE PROTECTION OF SHIPPING

The Range of Options

One thing as true of modern practice as it is of old, is that the protection of shipping involves a whole range of complementary activities between various kinds of threat. These activities include:

—convoy-and-escort, and/or its contemporary alternatives
—engagements against hostile units on the high seas
—attacks on the bases from which the raiders operate
—barrier operations against hostile units passing through geographic chokepoints on their way to attack shipping.
—mine counter-measures in coastal waters and harbour approaches.
—self-defence measures for merchant ships.
—if possible, attacks on the raiders' places of manufacture and support.

All these are operational approaches to the problem of protecting shipping from hostile attack. They would also be complemented by a series of non-operational measures such as the military regulation of the shipping industry, the construction and maintenance of the necessary number of appropriate ships and the prepositioning of military stocks in the required area before the conflict began.

The precise balance to be struck between these various options would depend on narrowly technical and professional matters specific to particular types of war situation. It would be, in other words, 'scenario-specific.'

CONVOYS AND TECHNOLOGY

Probably the most controversial aspect of the case would be the debate about the relative importance of the first of the alternatives listed above, namely convoy-and-escort when compared to other methods of defending shipping. This has always been a problem.

Convoys in Modern History

In the First World War, naval professionals in Britain put up a long resistance against the idea of introducing escorted convoys, and strongly preferred the alternatives. This was partly because Fleet commanders doubted whether they had enough escorts to make convoys safe unless they stripped the main battlefleet of essential destroyers; they thought that the best way to protect shipping was to destroy the forces that might threaten it most and the best way to do that was to force a decisive battle on the enemy's main fleet. Moreover, they pointed out that the actual process of forming convoys caused considerable delay and effective ship-loss. Finally, they doubted whether merchant seamen had the necessary skills to sail in close company anyway.

Few such doubts survived the near-catastrophe of the Spring of 1917, when the failure of alternative methods made the introduction of convoys an imperative. Thus, when World War II came, convoys were instituted without much argument. Once again though, they were but one of a whole variety of protective measures, most of which had important supportive roles to play.

In World War II, merchant shipping was mined and attacked by aircraft, submarines and surface ships. Submarines again proved to be the worst of the threats encountered:

TABLE 8.2: *World War II: The Submarine Campaign Against Shipping*

Period	Number of German U-Boats in Fleet*		German & Italian U-Boats Lost		Merchant Ships Sunk by U-Boats (Both German & Italian)		Ships Sunk Per Submarine Lost	
	Beginning of Period	End of period	German	Italian	Number	Tonnage	Number	Tonnage
1914–1918	20	121	178	NA	4,837	11,135,000	27.2	62,556
Sep 39–Dec 40	57	90	31	20	542†	2,500,000	10.6	49,020
Jan 41–Dec 41	90	248	35	18	427	2,400,000	8.1	45,283
Jan 42–Dec 42	248	398	87	22	1,155	6,500,000	10.6	59,633
Jan 43–Dec 43	398	440	237	25	462	1,500,000	1.8	5,725
Jan 44–Dec 44	440	425	239	NA	132	1,300,000	0.5	5,439
Jan 45–May 45	425	425**	153	NA	54	300,000	0.35	1,960
Sep 39–May 45	57	425***	782	85	2,772	14,500,000	3.2	16,724

*Normally less than one-half of U-Boats in fleet were operational at any one time.
**Figures unreliable for 1945. Generally, from 1943 to end of war, new construction of U-Boats kept up to losses.
***Total number of U-Boats produced from June, 1935, to May, 1945, was 1158.
†98 of these were sunk in the first four months of the war, 3 Sept.–31 Dec. 1939, and 155 in the next six months, to 30 June, 1940. In the last six months of 1940, after Norwegian and French bases were available to them the U-boats sank the other 289 ships destroyed during this period.
(Source: Rear-Admiral Sayre A. Swarztrauter *The Potential Battle of the Atlantic*. Proceedings of US Naval Institute, May 1979.)

Of course, once again, convoy-and-escort was far from being the only effective way of defeating submarines, aircraft and surface ships. Of the alternatives, the most important were the effective use of naval intelligence, the provision of air cover for convoys, anti-submarine patrols by Coastal Command and, most importantly, the effective use of allied industrial resources to build more merchant ships than German submarines could sink. By all these measures and by the application of intense technological effort into the design, manufacture and effective use of anti-submarine weaponry and detection systems (based, importantly, on techniques proved by operational research), the submarine was eventually defeated.

TABLE 8.3 *Analysis of German U-Boats Sunk 1939–45*

Cause		Total
Attack by:		
Surface		
Warship		246
Shore-based		
aircraft		245
Ship-borne		
aircraft		43
Shared kills:		
shore/ship	2	
aircraft		
ship/shore		
aircraft	33	
ship/ship		
aircraft	15	50
Submarines		21
Bombing raids		62
Mines		25
Other causes		64
Unknown		29
Total		785

(Source: S. W. Roskill, *The War at Sea Vol. III Pt. II.*
London: HMSO, 1961, p. 472.)

Lessons of World War II

The experience of World War II proved that submarines could have near-decisive strategic and tactical effects, and certainly occupied the attention of vast numbers of ships and aircraft. On this basis, as Admiral Gorshkov has remarked:

> Therefore the question of the ratio of submarine to anti-submarine forces is of great interest even under present-day conditions, since if ASW forces, which were so numerous and technically up to date (for that time), possessing a vast superiority, turned out to be capable of only partially limiting the operations of diesel submarines, then what must this superiority be today in order to counter nuclear powered submarines, whose combat capabilities cannot be compared with the capabilities of World War II-era submarines?

Contemporary Doubts about Convoy

As we have seen, one of the most striking effects of modern technology has been the rise in potency of the contemporary submarine. Whether they are nuclear or diesel-propelled, and armed with torpedoes or missiles, submarines are now much faster, better armed and capable of finding their targets than they were in World War II.

According to some experts, this means that convoys are much less valuable than they used to be as a way of protecting shipping. Amongst the reasons put forward for this are:

—modern surveillance systems, such as reconnaissance satellites, mean that convoys are no longer a good way of reducing encounter probabilities. Once, it made sense to sail ships in company, even if unescorted, since the convoys' horizon of visibility was much less than the sum of those of an equivalent number of ships sailing independently. Independent sailings simply multiplied the number of potential targets, thereby increasing encounter probabilities.

Nowadays, convoys cannot hide, and indeed are more open to detection by

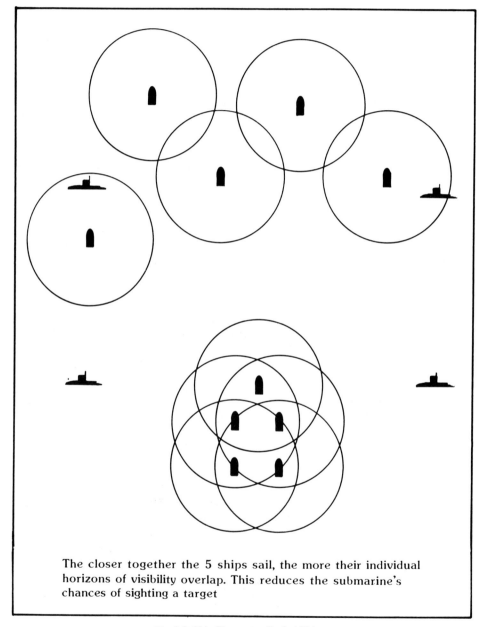

The closer together the 5 ships sail, the more their individual horizons of visibility overlap. This reduces the submarine's chances of sighting a target

FIG 8.2 Ship Encounter Probabilities.

satellite and other means than are individual ships. The ship might therefore be more, rather than less, vulnerable to detection if it sails in company.

—Modern submarines can now easily keep up with convoys. Moreover they are armed with potentially more lethal weaponry. Accordingly, an individual submarine can do more harm to a convoy than could its World War II predecessor, thus increasing the substance of the old 'all the eggs in one basket' objections to convoy.

—technology has also extended the air and subsurface threat by adding long-range missiles to the already serious threat posed by torpedoes. Some, as we have seen, doubt the surface escort's capacity to protect itself from such threats, let alone the merchant ships in its vicinity. Moreover, the number of escorts available is often said by NATO Fleet Commanders to be barely half of the number required. Finally, many modern warships have much less endurance than large, fast merchant ships.

—technology has also transformed the general strategic situation in various decisive ways. As we have seen, some doubt the whole validity of the idea of reinforcement shipping in the nuclear age anyway. Some of them say moreover, that convoying would be an especially unwise tactic since it might be the very thing that would tempt an aggressor to go nuclear in the first place. Moreover, technology effects the land battle too, and the situation on the Central Front, for example, could be so bad as to require fast, independent sailings, irrespective of whether this is, or is not, the safest operational method of getting reinforcements across the Atlantic. Here, naval operations would be determined less by what goes on at sea than by the nature of the fighting ashore.

Conclusions

In short, critics of the convoy-and-escort method of protecting shipping argue that the relentless march of technology has produced better surveillance systems and more capable submarines and aircraft, making this tactic less attractive than it used to be. This conclusion is reinforced by a number of non-naval arguments as well.

Needless to say, convoy-and-escort has at least as many defenders as it has critics. The defenders argue that the technology which has improved the means of attack has also increased the powers of defence. Surveillance satellites can be fooled by electronic and other counter-measures, and can be subjected to various means of anti-satellite attack. Point and area defence systems have improved in parallel with aircraft and submarine attack capabilities. And so the argument goes on!

Many of these themes will be addressed more substantively later in this series. At this stage all we need to do is note that technology has affected the role of defending shipping in a bewildering variety of ways and it is far from certain what the overall outcome would be. Certainly there are a great many ambiguous variables in the equation, whose effect depends very much on the scenario. Although it may not be possible, therefore, to predict what the precise balance between the various means of defence would be in any particular situation, we can be reasonably certain that the task of protecting shipping will continue to require a very wide mix of capabilities and strategies.

ELEMENTS OF THE MODERN BATTLE FOR SHIPPING

Amongst the variables concerned in any modern battle to attack or defend shipping would be:

The Numbers Involved

Both for the attacker and the defender, the number of ships, aircraft and submarines available for the campaign would depend first on the overall force-level and secondly on the consequences of whatever was happening elsewhere. In an East-West conflict in the Atlantic, for instance, the 140 or so torpedo or missile firing submarines of the Soviet Northern Fleet would theoretically be available to lead the attack. Estimates as to how many *would* actually be so used vary widely, and reflect differing judgements about the extent to which the Northern Fleet's other tasks would require submarines. The same thing would apply of course to Western forces.

Geography of the Battle Area

The configuration of the ocean floor, the water and the coastline would all be highly relevant to the course of the battle. The comparative distance between the battle area and the bases used by both sides would be especially important. Many of these variables can be positively exploited by the protagonists. They can make the maximum tactical use of water and weather conditions for example. Soviet problems would be increased if the West decided to send its shipping across the Atlantic on a southern route terminating in the Azores. On the other hand, a Soviet advance into Northern Norway would clearly help it to conduct a more effective campaign in the Atlantic.

Measures of Indirect Defence

Various types of action against the whole of the Northern Fleet should, in theory, reduce the number of hostile forces deployed against NATO shipping in the Atlantic. This is how a recent Supreme Allied Commander Atlantic (SACLANT) has described these measures:

> The method of control most likely to be effective against SACLANT's major threat, the submarine, will be a mixture of forward ASW barriers to control the choke points, attrition warfare against targets of opportunity that have escaped into the open sea, and offensive strikes against the enemy's ports and bases.

The balance that would be struck in allocating assets between these various measures of indirect defence, and indeed between them and the types of direct defence listed below, would be a matter of fine judgement on the day, and remains controversial. It is an area where computer-based campaign simulations would be particularly helpful.

Convoys

Most experts concede that convoys would have at least some part to play in a campaign to protect shipping. The size and shape of convoys would depend on the circumstances. At the top end of the scale a monster convoy of 300 ships on anti-nuclear spacing would be tens of miles broad and, especially, long. On the other hand, they might comprise a bare handful of especially valuable ships rushed across with the maximum protection.

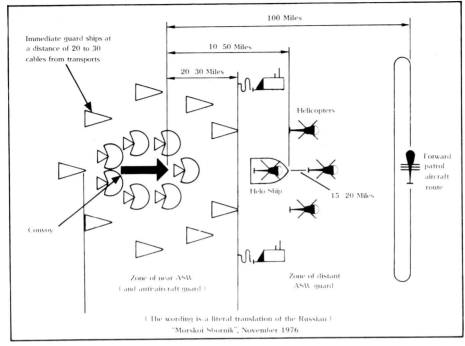

FIG 8.3 Convoy Tactics: The Soviet View.

Area Defence

Hostile attack might be expected to concentrate on places where geography reduces routing options, for example in narrows through which the shipping has to pass and in the approaches to the despatching and receiving countries. Defences might therefore be expected to coalesce around such areas in order to counter the resultant higher-than-usual concentration of enemy aircraft, submarines and perhaps surface ships.

Protected Lanes

This method stresses the defence of the sea areas through which shipping passes (or their 'sanitisation') rather than that of the shipping itself. The lane might, perhaps, be fifty miles broad. In the middle, there would be a two streams of independent ships, covered by bands of surface ships, helicopters, submarines and maritime patrol aircraft.

The advantage of the system is said to be the increase in tactical mobility and flexibility that would come from ships and submarines not having physically to escort merchant ships, which should lead to more effective prosecution of enemy submarines, not least because it means the engagement would tend to take place further away from noisy merchant ships. Moreover, independent sailings mean faster sailings, because ending the need to form convoys reduces turn-around time.

Critics of the scheme argue that protected lanes have never worked in the past, and, especially if they were long and expected to operate for sustained periods of time, would be so demanding in terms of the defensive assets they require as to undermine the effectiveness of other, better, methods.

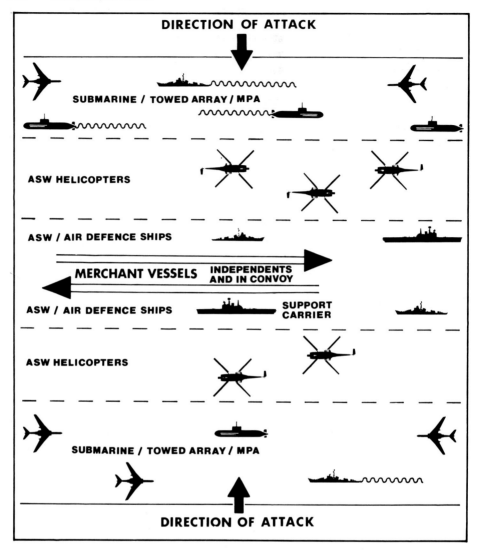

FIG 8.4 The Protected Lane.

Supporters argue that technology, especially in the shape of long range passive submarine detection systems, has made all the difference and the past is no guide.

Support Groups

A development of World War II practice, support groups are claimed to combine the advantages of convoy and protected lanes. Since this scheme envisages the use of smallish convoys (of perhaps forty ships with four escorts) merchant ships would be accorded a measure of direct protection and so would be able to spread themselves over a wider area than envisaged by the protected lane scheme. This should reduce the enemy submarine's chance of finding them.

At the same time, when buttressed by a large number of independent sailings,

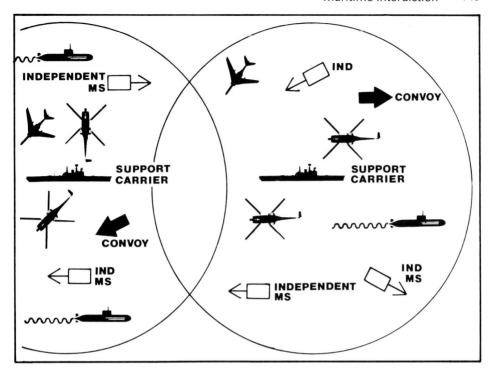

FIG 8.5 The Support Group.

these small convoys should benefit from the advantages of reduced sailing time provided by protected lanes. Moreover detached frigates, submarines and support carriers should not have the tactical disadvantages of having to operate in company with merchant ships.

Arming merchant ships

This has always played a part in the campaign to protect shipping and the Falklands campaign shows that it will very likely continue to be the case. The advance of technology has made available a range of containerised modular weapons systems which could, in theory, be placed on merchant ships as and when required.

However, this is not as easy an option as might appear to be the case at first glance. This policy would require large stocks of such weapons, and the infinite variety of the commercial merchant fleet (not least in mountings and power supplies) would make standardisation of equipment difficult. Maintenance could be a problem too. Finally, although there are modular weapons systems for air defence, such as *Phalanx* and *Goalkeeper*, there are fewer candidates for dealing with the submarine threat which is perhaps the more serious.

The Defence of Port Approaches

It must be expected that the shallow waters characteristic of the approaches to most of Europe's ports would see a great deal of activity from hostile diesel submarines, mines and, quite possibly, from aircraft. Dealing with this type of threat would require diverse defences comprising large numbers of small vessels and aircraft operating out of shore bases. It would be technologically difficult and would demand the most thorough knowledge of the topography of the ocean floor and of local water conditions.

However, this aspect of the protection of shipping cannot really be separated from the broader issues of inshore operations and it is to this that we will now turn.

9

Inshore Operations

Most of the world's navies spend most of their time operating within their own local waters carrying out a whole range of small scale, but nonetheless important, inshore tasks. These tasks have always been important, but developing technology has made them more so. Technology has, moreover, had some significant effects on the way in which they are carried out.

THE GROWING IMPORTANCE OF THE OFFSHORE ESTATE

The sea is more, not less, important than it used to be because it is a vital new source of food, energy and raw materials. Many of these marine resources, moreover, are to be found in the twelve mile territorial sea and the 200 mile Exclusive Economic Zone which most countries now claim off their coastlines.

Coal, oil and gas are extracted from the sea-bed in processes which have become central to the economies of many countries. At something like seventy million tons, the world fish catch is four times what it was a generation ago and is now an indispensable part of the protein requirements of an expanding world population, either directly as edible fish or indirectly in the shape of fertiliser. The sea-bed and, for that matter, sea water, are rich in an enormous range of minerals whose land supply is inevitably being reduced with each year that passes.

The sea is now even more important as a vehicle for the transportation of people, raw materials and manufactured goods than it used to be, and the busiest part of this traffic is found in port approaches and the narrow seas.

Finally, the sea has seen an extraordinary and world-wide rise in all manner of leisure pursuits, again mainly in the immediate offshore area. Marine tourism makes an important contribution to the economy of many countries.

The Need For Regulation and Control

All these important and varied uses of local seas are interdependent and inter-weave at all points. Thus, disturbance in one part of the system can have unlooked-for and deleterious effects on all the rest. The adverse effects on the fishing and tourist industries of marine pollution associated with oil extraction is only the most obvious example of this interdependence.

It follows from this that there is a growing need for more regulation at both the national and the international levels of all forms of sea use. This explains the world-wide increase there has been in the formulation of all manner of codes of practice relating to marine safety, health, welfare, law and order and environmental protection.

The value of offshore waters is such that countries have recognised a growing need physically to protect them, basically for three reasons:

(1).   Because so much may be at stake, there will always be the temptation for some users of the sea to attempt to evade the rules for economic advantage, and so there is a clear and growing need for expanding means of enforcement of agreed rules against the possibility of accident and against deliberate and conscious law-breaking

(2).   The fact that marine assets have become so valuable means they have become, more and more, the targets of disaffected groups of one sort or another. The growth of acts of marine terrorism (such as the hijacking in October 1985 of the liner *Achille Lauro*) clearly implies a need for more protection.

(3).   The value of offshore seas and technology-induced changes in the law of the sea have increased the possibility of dispute between neighbouring countries over the ownership of marine resources. This again implies a need for one country to defend what it sees as its marine interests against foreign nationals and governments who may not agree.

For all these reasons, the growth in economic importance of the offshore estate implies a need to regulate, control and, if necessary, protect it. This need has been accepted by many countries around the world.

As an example of the requirements faced by small nations, we may take the Bahamas. This country comprises hundreds of small islands and cays which are used more and more extensively by drug smugglers. In 1976, the Royal Bahamas Defence Force (RBDF) was forced to combat this menace, but soon found that its fifteen strong fleet of small patrol craft was insufficient for the task. More have therefore been ordered from foreign shipyards. To the cost of procuring these vessels must be added personnel, training and maintenance costs. On top of this there are problems with Cuba. In 1980, indeed, one of the RBDF's patrol boats was sunk by Cuban aircraft. The protection of its offshore estate is evidently a demanding task for small nations. Across the Caribbean, the burgeoning role of the US Coastguard shows that the same is true for larger ones.

THE MILITARY IMPORTANCE OF INSHORE WATERS

Inshore waters are militarily important for reasons over above their commercial value.

Coastal Defence

They may be used by the country which owns them to offer a kind of last ditch defence of the homeland against an incoming enemy, intent perhaps on making an amphibious landing or attacking land targets.

This localised form of sea denial is characteristic of very many countries. The Israeli Navy's 'peacetime' patrolling of its coastline against intruding Palestinian terrorists and wartime employment of small missile-armed attack craft in localised waters is a typical if particularly efficient example of the type.

In Europe, the navies of Denmark and Norway afford other examples. They go to great lengths to protect their long and vulnerable coastlines against overt or covert attack, by a kind of sea denial based on small boats, coastal artillery, defensive mining and the general exploitation of maritime geography. The potential of this form of defence was amply illustrated in 1950, during the Korean War in which the most powerful navy in the world was held up for weeks in its planned invasion of Wonsan by a few very ancient mines laid by the North Koreans.

The Soviet Union takes coastal defence very seriously too. Here the preferred method is to erect a system of concentric rings of defence, through which an enemy must penetrate in order to attack Soviet territory. The outer ring, perhaps some 1500 miles or so from shore, comprises all manner of submarines and long-range, land-based aircraft. Closer in, the attacker must expect to face major surface ships as well. Closer still to the shore, a swarm of minor combatants, torpedo boats and fast attack craft, mine fields and powerful coastal artillery will combine against him in the most unwelcoming way. A glance at the Soviet Navy's order of battle makes its perception of the importance of this task very clear.

Coastal Attack

Coastal attack is the mirror image of coastal defence. It comes in three varieties:

1. *Land Attack*

An intruder may seek to use the adversary's own waters as a base from which to bombard or launch amphibious attacks against the land. Some of these activities may well require the intruder's inshore forces to come along as well in order to deal with the defender's.

Nowadays such 'coastal' threats may be based on efficient sea-based aircraft and cruise missiles. For this reason, the task of defending the country against them becomes more and more demanding and less and less distinguishable from the kind of sea control operations we have already discussed.

2. *Coastal Sea Control/Denial*

This is really a coastal variant of the normal sea control/denial operations we addressed in Chapter 5. It amounts to one side trying to prevent the other from making full use of his own seas. Such operations often take the form of an attempt to prevent the enemy's naval forces (be they surface ships, conventional submarines, or for that matter ballistic missile firing submarines) from reaching their operational areas on the open ocean.

The possibility of this kind of hostile action in a country's own waters is the reason why naval professionals (especially American ones!) talk of the need to 'sanitise' the exits from their ports and bases before their main forces go to sea. The naval battles of the various Arab-Israeli and Indo-Pakistan wars were fought almost exclusively in these terms and remind us how common is this type of action.

3. *Offensive Mining*

Offensive mining of ships arriving at or departing from focal points and port approaches is really a particular form of coastal sea denial. But it deserves separate treatment because the fact that mines have been used in a recognisable form since the Crimean War sometimes tends to obscure the modern potential of this type of weapon. Probably about one and a half million of these have been laid all told, and at least half a million since 1945.

Mines can be easily deployed from surface ships and submarines, and indeed many of them are constructed with a twenty-one inch diameter so they can be fired from standard torpedo tubes. They can be dropped from aircraft, speed-boats or merchant ships. These days, they are very sophisticated indeed. They may be set off by physical contact, by the magnetic, acoustic or pressure influence of their target, or indeed by any combination of the three. They may be, and indeed usually are, deployed as a mixed bag in order to make the defender's task as difficult as possible.

Recent technological advances mean that mines can have a ship-count device, so they can let a number pass by before being activated. Their sensitivity and lethality can both be adjusted to suit the circumstances, and they can remain under the control of the country that deployed them for years if need be. On the termination of the Vietnam War, for example, it soon became clear that only the Americans could clear the mines they laid off Haiphong harbour, which in due course they duly did.

PLATE 9.1 Mines can be delivered in many ways, often using platforms designed for something else. Here a converted American *Hercules* drops a dummy mine in a test for the US Navy. Sea-bed mines are usually about 6′ long and 2′ in diameter. (Lockheed)

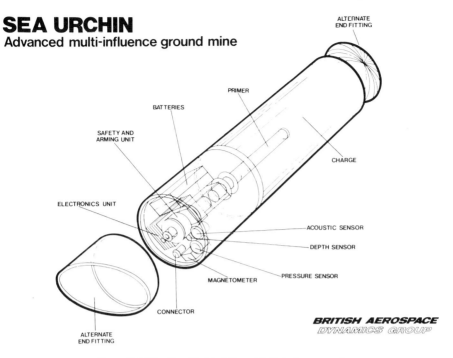

SEA URCHIN
Advanced multi-influence ground mine

ALTERNATE
END FITTING

PRIMER

BATTERIES

SAFETY AND
ARMING UNIT

CHARGE

ELECTRONICS UNIT

ACOUSTIC SENSOR

DEPTH SENSOR

PRESSURE SENSOR

MAGNETOMETER

CONNECTOR

BRITISH AEROSPACE
DYNAMICS GROUP

ALTERNATE
END FITTING

PLATE 9.2 The Sea Urchin Mine. (British Aerospace)

Nonetheless, these technological advances, expensive though they may seem, have not robbed the mine of its traditional cost-effectiveness. Nowadays this derives from three things:

—Maritime powers are very vulnerable to this kind of attack both in peace and war because they are so dependent on the sea. Modern ships, moreover, are a good deal less sturdy in constructional terms than they used to be.

—Mines have always been cost-effective in the sense that it costs a good deal more to clear or counter them than it does to deploy them. There is every sign that modern mining continues to call for a disproportionate response.

—Despite their technological sophistication, they still remain far cheaper than other weapons, like naval missiles, for example. It is difficult to offer

PLATE 9.3 The Sea Urchin Mine. (British Aerospace)

precise figures about this but for the cost of one *Harpoon* missile, the US Navy could probably afford up to several dozen effective mines.

For all these reasons, the offensive mining threat has become one of the serious forms of coastal attack.

REQUIREMENTS OF INSHORE OPERATIONS

Mine Counter-Measures

Mine warfare is a constant and never-ending battle of wits between tacticians and scientists on both sides. There is every sign that this battle will become more rather than less intense, and will make increasing demands on the technological capabilities of both sides.

In broad terms, mine counter-measures (MCM) involves three mutually supporting kinds of response:

1. *Tactical Response*

Having local command of the sea of course, may prevent the enemy from laying mines in the first place, and so would be the ideal tactical solution to the problem. It is, moreover, perfectly conceivable that the defender may, so to speak, mine the enemy minelayer out by the defensive mining of his own waters!

Minewatching, that is the constant monitoring of possible minelayers, or of the areas in which they might operate, may still make an important contribution since it narrows the field of search. Included within this surveillance function would be the maintenance of familiarity with the sea bottom. During the Red Sea mine clearance exercise in 1984, the bottom was found to be littered with metallic junk of all kinds, which considerably increased the complexity of the MCM task. Obviously, the more the local sea-bed is mapped and cleaned, the easier would be MCM in wartime.

Once the presence of mines is suspected however, traffic will certainly be regulated to pass through the safest waters available. Individual ships may be 'wiped', 'de-permed' or 'de-gaussed' (just as they were in 1939–45) to reduce their magnetic signature. If ships in dangerous waters proceed at slow speed, they reduce both their acoustic and pressure signatures as well.

2. *Minesweeping*

Minesweeping may be a *mechanical* activity aimed at physically cutting the mooring wires that tether some kinds of mine to the sea-bed. The more complex variant of minesweeping, however, is that which seeks to cause the mines to explode by simulating whatever influence (acoustic, magnetic, pressure, or any combination of the three) for which they have been designed. Arguably, even by the end of the Second World War, this had proved to be technologically too demanding, but some developments since then have improved the prospects for influence minesweeping. Such a one would be the *Troika* system currently operated by the West German Navy; this system has one control ship operating three small unmanned craft which simulate a variety of acoustic, magnetic and pressure signatures.

All the same, many experts believe that minesweeping is likely to grow more rather than less difficult in the future.

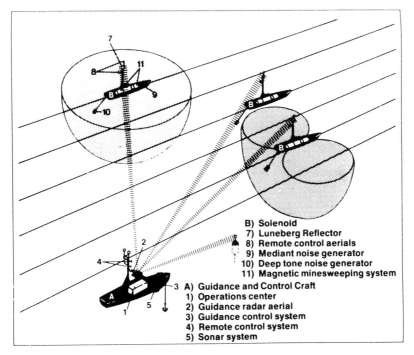

B) Solenoid
  7) Luneberg Reflector
  8) Remote control aerials
  9) Mediant noise generator
 10) Deep tone noise generator
 11) Magnetic minesweeping system
A) Guidance and Control Craft
  1) Operations center
  2) Guidance radar aerial
  3) Guidance control system
  4) Remote control system
  5) Sonar system

PLATE 9.4 The West German *Troika* minesweeping system has one central command ship controlling three unmanned platforms. (Navy International)

3. *Minehunting*

Although minehunting is slow, tactically difficult and tends to be dependent on good weather, it offers a valuable alternative to minesweeping. In general terms, the process starts by the use of active, high definition sonar to detect the possible presence of mines. Divers, or remotely operated vehicles will then be sent down to confirm the presence of the mine and determine the appropriate response. In many cases, the mine will be counter-mined, and simply blown up.

Clearing an area one mine at a time may prove to be a laborious and difficult job. Moreover, it is an area where technology helps the mine at least as much as it does the minehunter. For instance, detection sonar can be countered by camouflage, anechoic coatings which absorb sonar emissions, or even by fitting a vibrating mechanism which allows the mine to bury itself in the sea-bed. Despite the problems, however, minehunting is an essential part of the MCM effort.

Even though MCM forces tend often to be more neglected than other more glamorous naval forces, they are universally regarded as one of the most important constituents of all types of inshore operations. The burgeoning technological demands of the job mean that it is becoming more difficult to do. In mid 1984 one ship-load of mines were laid in the approaches to the Red Sea and it took eighteen MCM ships from six different nations, together with eight large helicopters and many support craft, many weeks to clear the area. The Italian contingent alone logged 480 minelike objects which had to be investigated (all of which turned out to be part of

PLATE 9.5 The West German *Pinguin B3* is a remotely controlled underwater craft which can be sent out to identify a suspected mine, locate and then destroy it with a counter-mining charge. (MBB/VFW)

PLATE 9.6 A counter-mining charge. These usually contain about 100 kg of explosive, aim to destroy the mine's electronics but sometimes set it off. (MISAR)

PLATE 9.7 The 238 ton West German minehunter *Loreley*. (FGN)

the tremendous litter modern man chooses to dump on the sea-bed). Because it is technically difficult to do, MCM is becoming more expensive. The price of the British *Hunt* class of minehunter is reported to be in the vicinity of thirty-five million pounds each, for instance. Nevertheless, the scale of the modern mine threat is such that few doubt the need for such counters.

Land-based defences

Historically, land-based forces of various kinds have always formed the last ditch defence of territory against sea-based attack. This is now as true as ever. Coastal artillery, shore-based missiles and aircraft (including interceptors, strike aircraft, maritime patrol aircraft and ASW helicopters) all form important constituents of the inshore defences of many countries, such as those of Scandinavia, as we have seen. In addition, several of them maintain specialised amphibious forces whose task it would be to defend offshore islands and installations against attack. There is little sign that the relative importance of this task is any less than it was.

Coastal submarines

Small, modern diesel powered submarines, specifically designed for operations on and around the continental shelf, are a characteristic feature of many of the world's advanced but smaller navies. There is no doubt at all that their limited size and quietness makes them still a serious threat to much larger forces attempting to pass through the narrow waters in which they typically operate.

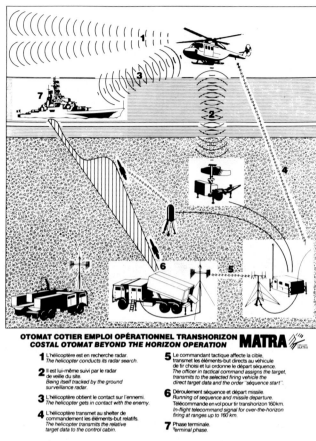

OTOMAT COTIER EMPLOI OPÉRATIONNEL TRANSHORIZON **MATRA**
COSTAL OTOMAT BEYOND THE HORIZON OPERATION

1 L'hélicoptère est en recherche radar.
The helicopter conducts its radar search.

2 Il est lui-même suivi par le radar
de veille du site.
*Being itself tracked by the ground
surveillance radar.*

3 L'hélicoptère obtient le contact sur l'ennemi.
The helicopter gets in contact with the enemy.

4 L'hélicoptère transmet au shelter de
commandement les éléments-but relatifs.
*The helicopter transmits the relative
target data to the control cabin.*

5 Le commandant tactique affecte la cible,
transmet les éléments-but directs au véhicule
de tir choisi et lui ordonne le départ séquence.
*The officer in tactical command assigns the target,
transmits to the selected firing vehicle the
direct target data and the order "séquence start".*

6 Déroulement séquence et départ missile.
Running of sequence and missile departure.
Télécommande en vol pour tir transhorizon 160km.
*In-flight telecommand signal for over-the-horizon
firing at ranges up to 160 km.*

7 Phase terminale.
Terminal phase.

PLATE 9.8 The *Otomat* land-based anti-ship missile
system. This diagram shows the helicopter searching for
a target with radar (1), being tracked by shore-based
radar (2) and locating a target (3). The helicopter sends
target acquisition information back to the control centre
(4). The Control Officer chooses the missile launcher
and transmits the target information (5). The missile is
launched (6) flies up to 160 km, ending its flight with a
low-level sea skimming approach and hits the target (7).
(Matra)

Small ships in large numbers

The increase of the territorial sea from three to twelve miles (and in some cases to
far more than this) and the acceptance of the idea of an Exclusive Economic Zone of
no less than 200 miles has enormously increased the sea area which navies must
defend. Despite the increase in range of many naval sensors and weapons, and the
widespread assistance now available from shore-based aircraft, there is an objective
need for more ships, simply to cover the area.

Most countries maintain a substantial fleet of small patrol craft of up to fifty tons or
so displacement. Many of these are so unmilitary in role and appearance that they are
not even operated by the naval authorities. Nonetheless, they perform a myriad of

PLATE 9.9 The launching platform for the very long range *Otomat* anti-ship missile system.
(Matra)

minor tasks associated with the regulation and protection of waters within, typically, one day's sailing of their bases. They may well be equipped with a light gun for law enforcement against the recalcitrant.

The Fast Attack Craft (FAC) which ranges from fifty to 500 tons in displacement is, in itself, a familiar component of modern naval warfare. In the Second World War, it took the form of the Motor Torpedo Boat (MTB). MTBs were used in narrow waters like the English Channel to attack enemy merchantmen or warships with torpedoes. They were fast, being capable of dash speeds of up to forty knots, and, though noisy, were often able to take advantage of darkness or bad weather to pose a significant threat of sea denial even against much larger ships.

Since then, four important technological developments have guaranteed the survival of the type:

—First, the miniaturisation of weapons has enhanced the offensive power of small craft vis-a-vis large ones, but has done so at reasonable cost in terms of capital, maintenance and manpower.
—Secondly, the sinking of the Israeli destroyed *Eilat* by Egyptian FAC armed with *Styx* missiles in 1967 confirmed the importance of the arrival of long-range naval missiles. This has increased the range at which the FAC can be effective and reduced its requirements in speed and stability. In the past, the small size of the FAC severely limited the size of its main armament and the accuracy with

which it could be fired. For the first time, the small ship can now operate the same weapon as the big ones.

—Thirdly, there have been many important though perhaps less dramatic improvements in all aspects of the construction and equipment of FAC, including the development of lightweight, unmanned medium calibre guns of extraordinary accuracy, effective, new lightweight torpedoes, the arrival of high speed diesel engines offering more in the way of range, better crew accommodation, and even a degree of air-defence with passive counter-measures (such as a reduction in silhouette to reduce the radar signature) and point-defences. All of these have vastly improved the capacity of the FAC. Some experts believe that in the longer term, FACs with unconventional hull-forms like hovercraft

PLATE 9.10 The *OTO Melara* Standard 76 mm gun is a rapid-firing gun, capable of firing 100 rounds a minute. It is to be found on many different types of warship. (Navy International)

PLATE 9.11 Attention has been paid by the *Saettia*'s designers to reduce the radar signature by a low silhouette, extensive use of non-metallic materials and sloping sides. (Navy International)

PLATE 9.12 As above.

or hydrofoils, will be the main source of significant improvement in the future.

—Fourthly, the modularisation of weapon and sensor systems means that FAC hulls can carry a wide range of alternative systems, which increases their unit and force flexibility a great deal.

Many of these characteristics are well illustrated by the modern Italian FAC the *Saettia*.

The speed, manoeuvrability, stealth, firepower and relative cheapness of the FAC means that they will continue to be a vital component of operations fought in the restricted waters of long coastlines, islands and archipelagoes. They are now very numerous in the world's navies and look set on remaining so.

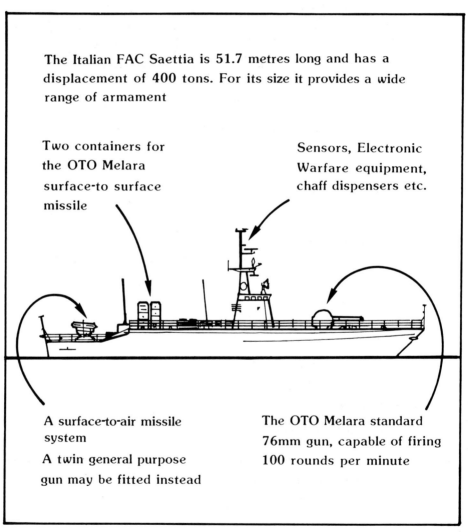

The Italian FAC Saettia is 51.7 metres long and has a displacement of 400 tons. For its size it provides a wide range of armament

Two containers for the OTO Melara surface-to surface missile

Sensors, Electronic Warfare equipment, chaff dispensers etc.

A surface-to-air missile system

A twin general purpose gun may be fitted instead

The OTO Melara standard 76mm gun, capable of firing 100 rounds per minute

Fig 9.1 The *Saettia*. (Source: Navy International)

The Saettia has more internal compartmentalisation than most FACs. This increases ship stability, damage control and crew comfort

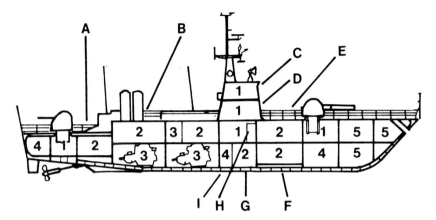

1 Weapons systems and operational spaces

2 Accomodation

3. Machinery spaces

4 Auxiliary machinery

5 Stores

A Berth for 6 ratings

B Crews mess to port, POs mess and galley to starboard

C Bridge

D Combat Information Centre

E Berths for 6 POs to starboard, single and double berths for officers to port

F Berths for 8 senior rates

G Berths for 9 ratings

H Radar room

I Stabilizing compartment

FIG 9.2 The *Saettia*, Internal. (Source: Navy International)

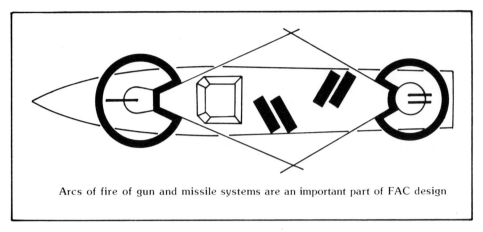

Arcs of fire of gun and missile systems are an important part of FAC design

FIG 9.3 The *Saettia*, Arcs of Fire. (Source: Navy International)

Nonetheless, they *are* basically restricted to the narrow waters, and their small size means that it is very difficult for them to operate helicopters, or to stay at sea for long periods; moreover, their ASW capacity is often very limited. These deficiencies have persuaded some countries of the need for a larger type of offshore patrol vessel to stiffen a force largely comprising FACs of various types. At the same time, there is a strong tendency for frigates to get larger, more complex and more expensive. In World War II, frigates were usually in the range of 1500–2500 tons, but now they go from 2000 tons up to 5000 in some cases.

For both these reasons, there has been something of a revival of the corvette type of ship of 800–1500 tons to fill this gap. In bluewater navies, its cheapness means larger numbers, and provides a useful back-up force for frigates and destroyers, especially in situations of reduced threat. For Third World navies, the corvette can act as a flagship for a navy of FACs and patrol craft, and can conduct naval diplomacy at appropriate levels. The characteristics usually envisaged for this type of ship include the capacity to operate up to 500 miles out for two weeks or more, adequate command and control, guns, anti-air defences and a missile, reasonable sea-keeping facilities and the ability to operate helicopters.

CONCLUSIONS

This review of inshore operations suggests that this is a type of naval operation which is becoming intrinsically more important because the waters in which it is conducted have themselves become more important for a complex web of political, economic and military reasons.

At the same time, the forces commonly used for such operations have, when aided by modern technology, developed formidable capacities which would make even a substantial naval force think very carefully before challenging them. Perhaps the consequence is some narrowing of the gap between small and large navies?

10

Naval Diplomacy

IMPORTANCE OF THE ROLE?

The fact that we will not be devoting much attention to the execution of this role should not be taken as evidence that it is not important. Instead, this lightness of treatment comes mainly from the fact that naval diplomacy is not a role for which navies are technically designed to any very significant extent. It is one carried out by ships which are designed fundamentally for something else.

Nevertheless, even in a book about the effects of technology on maritime strategy, some attention has to be paid to naval diplomacy because the prime task of all the world's navies, is not to fight wars but to prevent them. The advent of nuclear weapons and the high cost of even conventional warfare have been noted in the chapters above. The result is often said to be a discouragement of mankind's tendency to resort to wars (or at least full-scale ones) as a means of settling international disputes. This does not of course mean that the disputes themselves have gone away, but merely that the powers would prefer other ways of sorting them out.

It is here that naval diplomacy has come into its own, for navies seem to offer states a wide range of diplomatic instruments for use in normal peacetime, in times of strain and in times of crisis. Indeed, both American and Soviet maritime strategists argue that this, especially in the nuclear age, is one of the main justifications for having a navy in the first place. So important has naval diplomacy become, in fact, that it is one of the most widely studied aspects of contemporary naval theory and practice, as the final reading list shows.

THE NATURE OF NAVAL DIPLOMACY

Naval diplomacy is a label attached to the whole range of peacetime naval activities whose purpose is to influence the behaviour of other countries. At one end of the scale it might be quite coercive and involve the limited use of force. For examples of this, we may cite the recent activities of the United States Navy's 6th Fleet in the Mediterranean against Libya and certain interests in the Lebanon. Some recent analyses have identified over a hundred clear examples of the coercive application of force (or to give it its old title 'gunboat diplomacy') since 1945.

At the other end of the scale would be the gestures of support and friendship implied by routine joint exercises with other peoples' navies or courtesy visits to other peoples' ports. Because coercive naval diplomacy is so much more dramatic, it

PLATE 10.1 The Cod War between Iceland and Britain in 1976 was another example of naval forces used by both sides to transmit messages of resolve to each other. The wake in this picture shows that the Icelandic gunboat *Thor* has just turned sharply to port in front of the frigate *Leander* in a dangerous manoeuvre plainly intended to disrupt the British ship's effort to protect nearby trawlers. (MOD (Navy))

commands far more attention than standard exercises in showing the flag. But for all that, it is a far less common way of using naval power in peacetime as a way of influencing people.

The behaviour of the Soviet and American fleets during the Arab-Israeli War of 1973 is an interesting example of the wide range of options a naval presence can offer a country's leaders in times of crisis. During this war between the Superpowers' allies, both greatly increased the size of their fleets in the Mediterranean, basically for two reasons:

1.   They wanted to be able to provide their local allies with a degree of support in the fighting. Both sides therefore supplied large amounts of military equipment to the belligerents and protected it in transit.

2.   They wanted to transmit important messages to one another. Sometimes the message was a stern one indicating their resolve to help their local ally and a refusal to let the other interfere. From October 25–30th 1973 the United States declared a general nuclear alert, apparently because they believed the Soviet Union was about to intervene and wished to dissuade them. Accordingly the fleet moved into an area south of Crete and deployed its three carriers into a tight battle formation. To demonstrate *their* resolve, the Russians moved their forces into several surface attack groups aimed, so to speak, against the Americans.

On other occasions, both sides wanted to show a relaxation of tension, and did so by various means such as a physical move away from the battle area, the granting of shore leave and obvious reductions in readiness.

This widely studied example of naval diplomacy by both sides is generally thought to have been successful, and is certainly regarded as being much preferable to the kind of localised fighting that might have gone on in an earlier age.

The Diplomatic Advantages of Navies

It is not just naval officers but academic analysts and foreign policy specialists who say that navies are better at this type of diplomatic activity than the other services. The reasons they give for this often include:

—*Flexibility*. There are many different types of warship, and many of them are individually very versatile since they are equipped for a variety of operational tasks. Because of this, the same ship can be used to convey entirely different messages to adversaries or friends by the way it is used. Lights and canvas can transform the dourest man of war into a floating discotheque for visiting dignitaries in a matter of hours; a ship's geographical position is often used as a political signal and can easily be altered to suit the circumstances; the range of its weaponry provides a whole variety of diplomatic instruments. For all these reasons, it is hard to imagine a squadron of either aircraft or main battle tanks having the same diplomatic versatility as a modern warship.

—*Controllability*. Because warships can so easily be inserted into an area or withdrawn from it if events take an unpleasant turn, naval power limits the liability of those using it. In any case, there are fewer civilians at sea than on land, no cities and fewer state resources are tied up in it. A confrontation at sea is less sensitive, and less prone to accidental escalation, than a confrontation on land. For these reasons, the use of naval forces is usually regarded as less provocative, less dangerous and more controllable than that of their equivalents in the other services.

—*Strategic Mobility*. The slowness of ground formations, and the huge logistic difficulty of shifting them from one place to another is well known. Aircraft on the other hand, tend to be less mobile than they appear because they will often depend on the availability of routes over other people's countries and bases in them. Formations of warships, however, with supporting auxiliaries, can loiter in likely areas for weeks and sometimes months at a time, being on hand and on call. Despite the fact that they sail at far slower speeds than aircraft, sea-based forces are surprisingly often the first forces to appear at a trouble spot. In short, they are claimed to have more strategic mobility than the alternatives offered by the other services, and are often the best way of giving a country global reach.

DESIGNING A NAVY FOR DIPLOMACY?

It is, however, worth repeating that warships are not, so to speak, 'designed for' naval diplomacy. This is a by-product, and a kind of peacetime bonus, deriving

PLATE 10.2 Here the *Thor* runs into the stern of the *Andromeda*. The Icelandic gunboat was only some 900 tons, and had little in the way of armament. The *Andromeda* on the other hand was a powerful modern frigate of 2550 tons. Such collisions therefore had all the appearance of the strong bullying the weak. In fact, the sturdy Danish-built gunboat was much better suited to this kind of activity than expensive thin-skinned frigates, which usually came off worse, even though they could easily have blown the offending gunboat out of the water. The requirements of naval diplomacy may therefore differ widely from those of war-fighting. (MOD (Navy))

from their essential character as weapons of war. Ship designers can rarely afford to build into their designs characteristics which would be useful for diplomatic purposes (like large cocktail lounges) unless they have other more important functions as well.

But for all that, many experts argue that reinforcing or at least sustaining diplomatically useful characteristics like the flexibility, controllability and strategic mobility of naval forces would seem to be a sensible investment, other things being equal. This, for two reasons:

1.   In point of fact, naval forces are fortunately much more likely to have to do this than they are to fight wars! The more successful they are, moreover, the less chance there is of war.

2.   There is a certain tendency for the demands of war-fighting to diverge from those of diplomacy. For instance, it is widely believed that the relative war-fighting value of submarines has gone up, but their value for flag-showing is usually very limited. In the same way, naval missiles may be the weapon of battle but they have their limits as a means of warning errant trawlers or of firing salutes.

Attempting to preserve the diplomatic value of navies may well involve:

—maintaining numbers, because this helps both force flexibility and strategic mobility. More ships means more areas and situations covered.

—making sure that individual ships have as varied a fit of weapons on board as possible because this helps them cope with a wider range of situations. Very capable weapons may well turn out to be less useful than expected, because they are not appropriate to the particular situation. In this connection the re-appearance of the gun for the naval support of amphibious operations has been welcomed by those interested in the peacetime functions of navies.

—defending the controllability of naval forces by reducing the vulnerability of ships to surprise attack. As we have seen, this vulnerability sometimes drives naval officers to ask for permissive rules of engagement based on the notion of 'anticipatory self-defence' (i.e. attacking someone else is justified if he is believed to be on the point of attacking you). However understandable this may be, it reduces the controllability, and therefore the diplomatic value, of naval forces, especially in the kind of crisis when they are most needed.

—ensuring that professional sailors personally remain as good a set of ambassadors as they have always claimed to be. In some circumstances, the ability to entertain visiting dignitaries may serve the interests of the country at least as well as someone's capacity to shine in battle.

PLATE 10.3 Naval diplomacy, and the more general business of deterrence at sea, rests on close knowledge of the other side's activities. Considerable stress is therefore given to monitoring the naval operations of other countries and to the constant collection and processing of data about them. The Soviet bloc maintains a large fleet of naval-intelligence gatherers, or AGIs. This is the 245 ton East German *Meteor*. (MOD (Navy))

PLATE 10.4 Intelligence-gathering is largely a matter of electronic eavesdropping as the array of antennae on the *Meteor* suggests. (MOD (Navy))

—doing their best to make sure that warships continue to look impressive, for appearance still matters in international politics.

Unless there are serious operational penalties involved in so doing, navy planners and ship designers usually do their best to preserve characteristics like these from the effects of technological change, because they help navies perform roles in peacetime which have, fortunately, become ever more important.

11

Conclusions

The effects of technology on contemporary maritime strategy and on the roles and activities of the world's navies is simply too vast a topic to permit of any easy set of conclusions. There is a second reason for leaving such conclusions open, at least for the time being, and that is the fact that the impact of technology on sea power is not just the theme of this book, but of the series as a whole.

Nevertheless, even at this early stage, three very broad conclusions do seem to suggest themselves as worth bearing in mind when reading later volumes:

In the first place, and despite views to the contrary that were quite widespread a generation ago, at the onset of the nuclear age, there is very little sign that

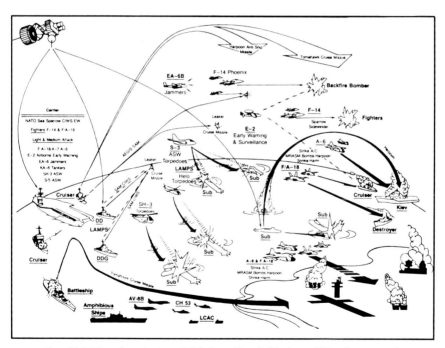

FIG 11.1 The Complexity of Modern Naval Warfare. This diagrammatic representation of forward operations by the US Navy (off NATO's northern flank?) illustrates the complexity and interconnectedness of maritime operations. Planning navies and understanding the way they work becomes ever more difficult. (Source: The Maritime Strategy, produced in January 1986 by the Proceedings of the US Naval Institute).

technological development has reduced the relative value of sea power. While some of its more traditional roles may have been fundamentally changed, or reduced in importance, other new ones have risen to take their place. Nor does this apply only to the great and established maritime powers. The proliferation of naval weaponry around the world, suggests that acceptance of the continuing, and maybe even increasing, importance of sea power is effectively global.

Secondly, and for all that, there remains much diversity of view about more detailed questions of how new technology has changed the way in which these roles, both old and new are best performed. It is tempting to compare this high level of uncertainty to the situation which existed in the last quarter of the 19th Century when industrialisation had produced so many new technical developments for navies, that professional sailors became really quite bewildered when they considered what the shape of future war at sea might be.

Finally, technology has increased the range of choice very considerably, but its high economic cost has, if anything, reduced the resources available. All maritime countries, whether they are large, medium or small, are therefore faced with the need to try to match resources and commitments in an uncertain world. All the signs are that the tasks of matching ends and means are not growing any easier.

It would seem from this that the impact of modern technology on sea power is widely relevant, generally important and very difficult to resolve. This reinforces the need to increase understanding of these issues amongst naval professionals, and among those interested in their ways, and it is hoped that both this volume and the series will make a contribution toward that end.

References and Further Reading

The following list of books is by no means a comprehensive one. It contains books that proved particularly useful for the compilation of this volume, and which should help the reader wanting to take these matters further.

Jonathan Alford (Ed), *Sea Power and Influence*. London: Gower for the International Institute for Strategic Studies, 1980.

Merrill L. Bartlett (Ed), *Assault from the Sea*. Annapolis, Maryland: Naval Institute Press, 1983.

K. Booth, *Navies and Foreign Policy*. London: Croom Helm, 1977.

James Cable, *Gunboat Diplomacy*. London: Macmillan, 1981.

Bradford Dismukes and James McConnell, *Soviet Naval Diplomacy*. New York: Pergamon Press, 1979.

James L. George (Ed), *Problems of Sea Power as We Approach the Twenty-First Century*. Washington: American Enterprise Institute, 1978.

S. G. Gorshkov, *The Sea Power of the State*. Oxford: Pergamon Press, 1979.

Hubert Moineville, *Naval Warfare Today and Tomorrow*. Oxford: Basil Blackwell, 1983.

Paul Nitze, *Securing the Seas*. Boulder, Col.: Westview Press, 1979.

Geoffrey Till, *Maritime Strategy and the Nuclear Age*. London: Macmillan, 1984.

Index